CREATIVE
RUG MAKING

Edited by Sue Simmons

Henry Regnery Company
Chicago

Crochet Abbreviations

alt	alternate(ly)
approx	approximately
beg	begin(ning)
ch	chain(s)
cont	continu(e) (ing)
dc	double crochet
dec	decrease
foll	follow(ing)
gr	group(s)
grm	gramme(s)
hdc	half double
in	inch(es)
inc	increase
No.	number
patt	pattern
rem	remain(ing)
rep	repeat
RS	right side of work
sc	single crochet
sl st	slip stitch in seaming
ss	slip stitch in crochet
st(s)	stitch(es)
tog	together
tr	treble
WS	wrong side of work
yo	yarn over hook

Edited by Sue Simmons

First published in Great Britain in 1976 by
Marshall Cavendish Publications Limited, London
First published in the United States in 1976 by
Henry Regnery Company
180 North Michigan Avenue, Chicago, Illinois 60601

Printed in Great Britain
International Standard Book Number: 0-8092-7999-1

Pictures supplied by

Malcolm Aird: 33
American Museum: 6(b)
Camera Press: 30/1, 41, 49, 54, 55, 70/1
Cooper-Bridgeman Library: 7(t)
Alan Duns: 38
Fabbri: 10, 11, 12, 14, 15
Su Gooders/Ardea: 7(b)
Michael Holford: 6(t)
Peter Kibbles: 46/7, 82
Chris Lewis: 43, 45, 56, 57, 62, 66/7, 76, 78
Mahoney: 86
La Maison de Marie Claire: 65
Julian Neilman: 68/9
Patons & Baldwins Ltd: 16, 18, 19, 22, 23
Ryagarn: 35
Transworld: 27, 44/5
Jerry Tubby: 26, 29, 36
V. & A. Museum Crown Copyright: 4/5
Rupert Watts: 60

Introduction

For centuries rugs have been used to add both warmth and color to the home. Nowadays it is possible to buy any number of machine-made rugs, but there is no better way to give any room an original finish than to add a rug designed and made by you.

Whether you have attempted rug making before, or you are a complete beginner, *Creative Rug Making* shows you how to work with a variety of techniques to obtain many different results – from the simple method of using a latchet hook to produce a warm pile effect to stitchmade rugs where the most ornate and delicate designs can be achieved. Here you will find how other traditional skills, such as crochet, can be used to create unusual rugs for any room in an unexpected variety of materials – soft rugs for the bedroom, strong sewn rugs for the playroom, tough, washable rag and braided rugs for working areas and a beautifully luxurious machine-knitted rug to enhance a living room.

Creative Rug Making contains lots of lavishly illustrated ideas and colorful patterns for you to make and adapt for your own home. So why not make yourself a rug and add an individual and personal touch to your surroundings.

Contents

Rugmaking through
the centuries   5

Hooked rugs   9

Plotting a
sunflower   14

Panel by panel –
a Japanese rug   17

Sun motif
floor cushion   26

Hooked
Oriental rug   28

Big bold lion
for the playroom   31

Long pile or
rya rugs   33

Diamond pattern
rug for beginners   35

Ripple
rya rug   37

A bright color-
blended rya rug   39

Stitch-made
tapestry rugs   41

Combining stitches –
a textured rug   47

A garland of roses   49

Tibetan poppy   54

Spacecraft in
stitches   56

Pompon rug   61

Multi-colored
braided rugs   62

Traditional
rag rug   66

Patchwork rug
from leftovers   69

Crochet a
durable rag rug   70

Circles and bands
crochet rug   73

Bathroom set
to crochet   75

For machine knitters –
luxury under foot   77

Play plan   79

Catch a tiger   82

Crochet square rug   86

Techniques for
rug design   87

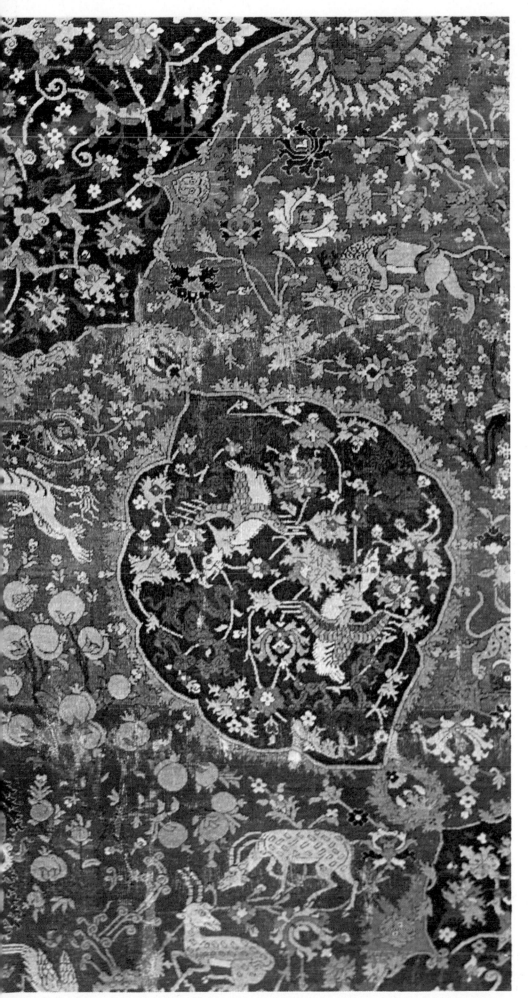

Rugmaking through the centuries

A cozy rug beside a cheerful fire – the ideal picture of warmth and luxury. Rugs have been with us for quite a few centuries now, making our lives more comfortable.

The oldest example in existence was found during excavations at Altai, on the Mongolian-Chinese border. Although it dates from about 500BC it is so expertly woven, with its borders of deer and mounted huntsmen, that the craft must have been well established even by that early date.

The skill flourished among the nomadic tribes of Asia, perhaps because rugs and carpets were some of the few furnishings possible in a tent. Each region, sometimes even each tribe, developed rugs that were characteristically their own. Each had an individual pattern for their rugs, completed a rug in a certain way, or used some different knot to work the yarn into the firm backing.

Emblems woven into jugs and carpets had a special significance. Pomegranates and camels stood for prosperity, dogs drove away evil, and so on. Colors too had their meanings, such as brown for fertility or red for joy and happiness. Wool was the most common material used, but rugs were also made from cotton, goat or camel hair, linen and, most luxurious of all, silk. The yarn was dyed with vegetable colors until about a hundred years ago when aniline dyes were introduced.

To the Moslems the rug became more than just a piece of furnishing. It was a private place for prayer, providing a small island of solitude no matter where the owner happened to find himself. Prayer rugs were often handed down from generation to generation. Many have a curve worked in the design at one end, to represent the dome of the Great Mosque at Mecca, and some have their date worked in Arabic numerals.

Left *A section from the Chelsea carpet, made in Persia during the sixteenth century when rugmaking had reached a peak of perfection.*

Rugs and carpets began to be introduced into Europe through the trade routes, or were brought home by returning Crusaders. As early as the 11th and 12th centuries they were being made in Spain, probably introduced by the Moorish invaders. But they were available only to the wealthiest people, and were used as table covers or as part of the trappings for a rich man's horse. Sometimes too, they were used as wall hangings. They were far too valuable to be trodden underfoot.

When Queen Eleanor of Castile came to England to marry Edward I in 1254, rugs were hung from windows as part of the decorations to greet her. Three hundred years later, rugs and carpets were still found only in the homes of the very wealthy. The Venetian Ambassador gave Cardinal Wolsey sixty Damascene carpets, and an inventory of the possessions of James V of Scotland lists many pieces of carpet, including some made of silk.

But European countries were not content with importing rugs, they wanted to make their own. In the early 18th century the first English factory, the Wilton Royal Carpet Factory, was set up. Soon after, others were established, often manned by Huguenot or Passavan weavers who had been forced to flee from France where they had been employed in carpet factories, because of religious persecution.

Rugs and carpets now came within the reach of a much wider market. There were still many homes though, where the budget would not stretch to such luxuries, so the women used their

Left *The tree of life is one of the richest and most popular of classical designs. Here it is woven into a Persian carpet made in Ghum.*
Below left *Patriotism was often the theme of rugs made in the United States.*
Below *An American landscape design in shades of green and brown.*

Above *This vividly colored Victorian English rug was worked in a simple embroidery cross stitch using a strong worsted thread.*
Right *Familiar scenes of everyday life are worked into the design on this modern rug made in Cairo.*

ingenuity and made their own. They used several different methods, each of which is as effective today as it was a couple of centuries ago.

Some copied the style (and often the patterns) of the professionals, and knotted strands of wool through a canvas or burlap backing. This gave warmth and softness.

Where economy was the watchword, women devised rugs from odds and ends of materials. Round or oval rugs made from braiding strips of stout material were popular in America, as were 'tongue' rugs, where pieces of thick fabric were overlapped on a firm base, then sewn down securely. There were knitted and crocheted rugs too, sometimes worked using several strands of wool at a time.

But the most popular rug in working-class homes during the 19th century must surely have been the hooked rug. 'Hooky', 'raggy', 'proggy' – it had many names up and down the country, but its manufacture was the same – simple and cheap. Made of strips of cloth hooked through a strong base, it was often rather somber in color, since the clothing of the day was usually

black or gray, with flashes of scarlet from winter flannel underwear, and the odd blue or green from a discarded apron. The rag bag in most homes could provide a couple of such rugs a year, and it was very satisfactory spring cleaning that could be completed with a fresh raggy mat to lay down before the kitchen range.

In England the patterns tended to be geometric, but in America they preferred a more pictorial approach. Landscapes, flowers and patriotic designs were very popular. The heyday of hooked rugs in America was probably

just after the Civil War, when an ex-soldier, Edward Sands Frost, hit upon the idea of selling rug canvas with the design already stenciled on it. This innovation spread all over the country, and similar rugs became so popular that they are now a part of the folk art of America.

Nowadays we can buy any amount of machine-made rugs and carpets, but for anyone who wants to add a touch of individuality to their home, to make something that is original and practical, then the handmade rug still offers plenty of scope.

Hooked rugs

Using cut wool with a latchet hook is one of the easiest and fastest ways of making a rug. The uncomplicated technique produces a warm and hard-wearing pile that will last for a lifetime and the only specialized tool needed is the latchet hook which is inexpensive and can be bought at the same store as the rug wool.

There are two main categories of hooked rugs – short pile or Turkey rugs and long pile, of which Rya rugs are an example. They are both worked in a similar fashion but there are slight differences in techniques and materials and so they are dealt with separately.

Short pile rugs

There are three possible ways to go about making a pile rug. You can buy a kit with the design already printed on the canvas and the correct amounts of yarn in each color included. These are very useful for traditional or complicated designs and some suppliers are now offering a service to make up your own design from your own sketch or photograph to your own requirements of color and size.

You can also buy a plain canvas with a charted design. These are slightly more complicated to work with because you have to count up the squares on the chart which indicate the parts of the pattern, and mark the canvas in a similar way. However, they do give you the chance to adapt the design and to choose your own color scheme.

If you are really adventurous, you can buy a strip of canvas and make a design of your own. It is best not to work too complicated a pattern to start with; subtle blends of color, worked in rows, often produce a simple yet attractive design. It is usually a good idea to rough out a scheme in advance because the rug should be worked in straight lines from one end.

What you need to make your rug
Canvas: This comes in various widths from $13\frac{3}{4}$ inches to 45 inches, so there is plenty of choice for whatever size rug

Left *A brilliantly colored rug worked in squares makes an ideal first project for the beginner.*

you make. A good size is 6 feet by 3 feet. The canvas you need is approximately 10 holes to 3 inches rug canvas.

Yarn: The correct yarn for short pile rugs is a coarse 6-ply rug yarn. This is available either in skeins which can be cut to whatever length you want by winding the yarn around a grooved wooden gauge (or a book of the appropriate size will work just as well) and then slicing along the groove with a sharp razor, or you can buy it precut in bundles of over 300 pieces. These are called units and one unit will cover 3 squares with a little to spare. For the overcast edge, buy skeins of yarn to match.

Tools: A latchet-hook is the only specialized tool you will need and is available from any needlework shop. Shaped like a large crochet hook with a wooden handle, it has a hinged latchet which closes the open end of the hook as you make the rug knot, and prevents the canvas from becoming entangled.

How to start
For a rug with straight sides, place the canvas on a table with the selvages on your left and right, and with its full length away from you. To make a neat, strong edge, turn up the cut end nearest you for about 1½ inches, with the holes matching the holes underneath. Baste it down in position. The first few rows of knots should be worked through the double thickness.

Skipping one square at the bottom and on each side of the canvas, start working the knots, one to each small square, from left to right, or right to left if you are left-handed.

For a circular rug, leave an unworked ¾-2 inches border around the edge.

The quickest knot to do is the 4-movement Turkish knot (Page 11). When completed, the tufts of the knot lie toward you. If two people are working the rug from opposite ends, one person should do the 5-movement knot (Page 11), in which the tufts lie away from the worker, so that the pile will run in the same direction down the length of the rug.

Fringes and finishes
When all the knots have been worked in the canvas, it is a good idea to add

Below *The tools necessary for making rugs.*

strength to the edges by finishing them. On square or rectangular rugs, all four sides can be finished by stitching or crocheting in one of the methods given below. Alternatively, two opposite sides – preferably those worked through the double layer of canvas – can be edged with a fringe. On a semi-circular rug, the straight edge should be finished by stitching and the curved edge in the same way as for a circular rug.

The rugs should never be backed – the open construction of the canvas is not visible from the pile side, yet allows any grit on the surface to work its way through to the back of the rug where it can be easily cleaned. Adding a backing would trap the dirt and make cleaning much more difficult.

Making a fringe
On rugs made by the classical method of weaving, the warp threads of the foundation (usually cotton or silk) are secured at each end by knotting them together about 4 – 6 inches from the ends in groups of four or five. You can achieve a similar effect on a canvas foundation by adding a fringe to the unworked thread each end of the canvas, using a latchet hook.

The fringe can be made from natural-colored or white cotton (use the type sold for knitting dishcloths), or from the wool used to finish the other edges. A multicolored fringe can be very effective, but on a rug with a strong pattern a plain one from one of the darker, background colors usually looks best.

The simplest method of cutting the lengths of yarn for the fringe is to find a book which is twice as deep as the required length of the fringe. Wind the yarn around it from top to bottom and cut through the threads along both edges.

Place the rug on your work surface with the pile facing up and the edge to which you are adding the fringe toward you. Weight the other end to prevent the rug from slipping.

Working from left to right, insert the hook under the first thread of canvas. Take three lengths of yarn and, treating them as one piece, fold them in half and loop them around the neck of the latchet hook. Complete the knot as for the 4-movement Turkish knot (Page 11), and pull the ends tight to secure it.

When all the knots have been worked, brush the ends towards you and trim off any uneven threads.

Finish off a circular rug
The only satisfactory method of finishing the edges of a circular or shaped rug is by binding it with matching 2 inches

The four movement method –

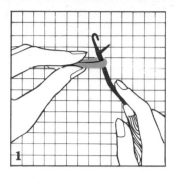

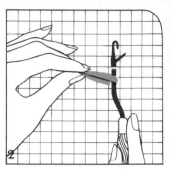

The four movement method of hooking is used when one person is making a rug. If two people are working, then one should use the five movement method.

1 *Fold a cut length of yarn in half and, holding it between the thumb and index finger of the left hand, loop it around the neck of the latchet hook.*

2 *Holding the ends of the yarn, insert the hook under the first of the horizontal weft threads.*

3 *Turning the hook a little to the right, take ends of yarn around the hook.*

4 *Pull the latchet hook under the weft thread and through the loop of yarn, catching the two ends in the hook as the latchet closes automatically.*

5 *Pull the ends of the yarn tight to check that the knot is firm. The tuft will finish up lying toward you.*

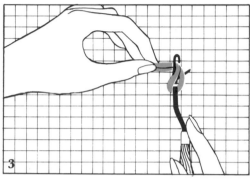

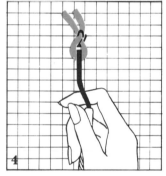

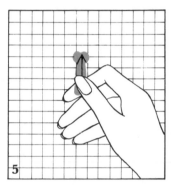

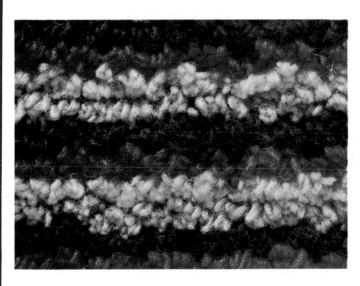

Above *Two simple but effective designs using combinations of colors in stripes*

The five movement method—

1 *Insert latchet hook under the first of the horizontal (weft) threads.*

2 *Loop the piece of yarn over the hook.*

3 *Pull the hook back through the canvas until the yarn loop is half-way through the hole, then push the hook through the loop until the latchet is clear.*

4 *Turn the hook, place the ends in crook and pull hook back through the loop.*

5 *Pull the knot tight.*

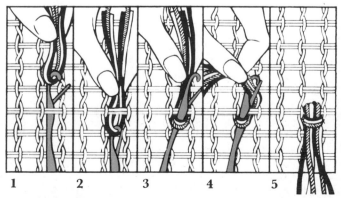

1   2   3   4   5

carpet braid. You need enough to fit around the edge of the rug, plus about 2 inches for turnings.

Start by trimming the unworked border of the rug to 1¾ inches, then press this section down onto the 'wrong' side of the rug, so that the outer edge of the braid is slightly inset from the edge of the carpet. Make darts on the inner edge of the braid where necessary (Figs 1–3).

Using strong carpet thread, overcast the tape to the canvas along both edges and stitch down the darts.

Stitched edge

If you are finishing all the sides by stitching, work the ends which have the doubled canvas first and then do the selvages. For all the methods of stitching you should use a carpet needle with a large eye and skeins of rug wool in a shade to match or blend with the color at the edge or background of the rug. You cannot use the standard ready-made packs of wool for this.

Overcasting or plaited stitch

This can be worked from left to right (Fig 4) or right to left.

To work from left to right, have the back of the rug facing up and the edge you are stitching away from you. Darn in the end of the wool and work a few overcast stitches in the first hole and over the outside thread of canvas. Pull the wool through the hole toward you, move to the fourth hole, taking the wool over the outside canvas thread, and through the hole toward you again. Take the wool over the canvas thread at the top of the fourth hole, go back to the second hole and pull the wool out toward you. Take the wool over the canvas thread and insert in the fifth hole, pull out toward you, take over the canvas thread and insert in the third hole. Continue along the whole side in this way.

To work from right to left, have the pile side uppermost and the edge you are stitching away from you. The needle should always pass from the back of the canvas to the front.

Insert the needle into the first hole from the back of the rug and pull the wool through, leaving a tail of about 3 inches lying along the top edge to the left. This will be covered by the stitches as you work. Holding the tail with your left hand, take the wool over the outside canvas thread to the back and insert it into the second hole. Pull the wool through, take it over the edge to the back of the canvas and insert it through the first hole again.

Take the wool over the edge and insert the needle from the back into the fourth hole. Take it over the edge to the back and insert it into the second hole again.

Continue working in this way, forward three holes and back two holes each time. To go around a corner, go back two holes, forward two, back one, forward one, then continue on the second edge as for the first one.

Blanket stitch

This is worked from left to right with the edge placed nearest to you and the pile side uppermost. Make two stitches in each hole (Fig. 5).

Insert the needle into the first hole from the pile side and pull through to the back of the carpet, leaving a tail of wool about 3 inches long. Hold the tail to the right so that it will be covered by the next stitches, then insert the needle into the same hole from the pile side. Pull it out, taking it under the outside canvas thread from the back of the rug and through the loop of wool. Pull tightly to secure the stitch.

Cable stitch

This is like a reverse blanket stitch. It is worked from right to left, with the edge placed nearest to you and the pile side uppermost.

Insert the needle into the first hole from the pile side and pull through leaving a tail of about 3 inches long. Hold the tail toward you with the needle on its left. Bring the needle over the tail to the right and insert it through the loop of wool made at the edge of the canvas. Still holding the tail, pull up the wool to secure the stitch. The tail can now be left free to be darned in later or you can continue holding it to the left to be covered by following stitches.

To make the second stitch, make a loop by holding the part of the wool which is nearest the first stitch over to the left. Insert the needle into the hole from the pile side and pull it out, taking it under the outside canvas thread from the back of the rug and through the loop of wool. Pull up the stitch firmly (Figs 10–11). Make all the following stitches in the same way.

Crochet edging

This is worked from right to left with the pile side uppermost and the edge placed away from you. One stitch is made in each hole.

Using a J or #10 crochet hook, push the hook through the first hole and pull through a loop of wool, leaving a long tail to be darned in later. Keeping this loop on the hook, catch the wool from the back over the edge of the canvas and pull through the loop. Keep the loop thus made on the hook. To make the second stitch, put the hook into the next hole from the pile side, catch the wool from the back and pull it through the hole. Keeping the loops on the hook, catch the wool again over the edge of the canvas and pull it through the two loops on the hook. Push the hook through the third hole and repeat the second stitch (Fig. 6–9) and so on.

Below *Detailed view of fringing worked at the short end of a rectangular rug*

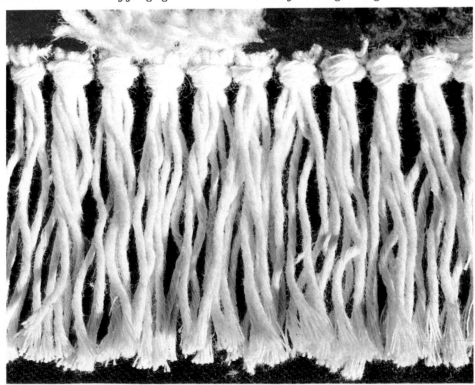

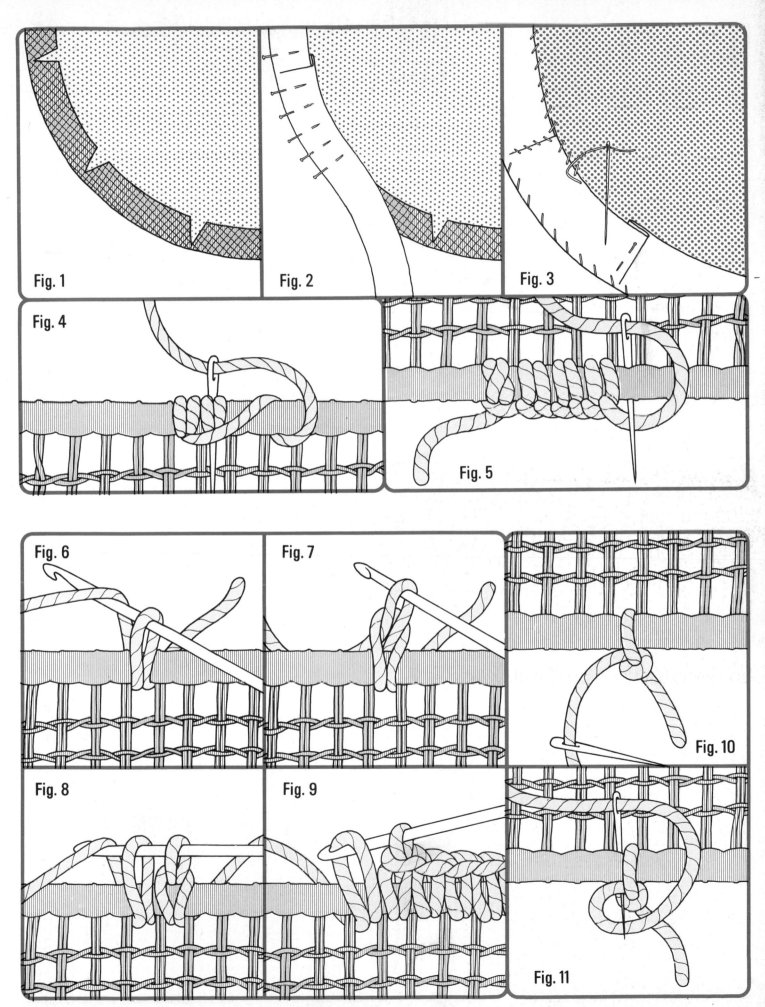

Fig. 1

Fig. 2

Fig. 3

Fig. 4

Fig. 5

Fig. 6

Fig. 7

Fig. 8

Fig. 9

Fig. 10

Fig. 11

Plotting a sunflower

Plotting the design of a rug from a chart onto the canvas needs care. For complicated designs, a canvas with the pattern already stenciled on it is ideal. If you plot your own pattern, remember that it will show the color of the stitches in the holes, whereas the actual stitches are worked on the lines of the canvas.

How to work and adapt the chart

If you are using a chart, it makes it easier if you first mark the design onto the canvas with a felt pen. Draw a vertical line down the center of the canvas from which to work the pattern. To mark the base of the stalk, count six rows up from the bottom of the canvas, (after folding over a hem of 1½ inches), and mark the two middle holes, that is, the ones immediately on either side of the center line. Then, following the chart, count up the holes and mark the design on the canvas. It will simplify later work if the color changes on the chart are marked with a corresponding felt pen on the canvas.

Once you have grasped the basic idea of the pattern, you can alter it to fit your own canvas. One flower, two leaves and a stalk take 1018 holes and 4 units. Work out the total number of holes in the canvas (width holes multiplied by length holes) and subtract from it the number for each flower or flowers. This will give you the background number. Divide this number by 320 (the number of pieces of wool in a unit) to give you the number of wool units you need for the background color. Remember to subtract the number of flowers you want to work on your canvas from the total number of holes.

Materials required

To make a rug measuring 2 feet square, you will need:

Canvas 2 feet wide, 27 inches long, to allow an extra 1½ inches at each end to turn under.

Yarn total 6400 holes (80 x 80)
red – 1 unit (231 holes)
yellow — 1 unit (294 holes)
green – 2 units (493 holes)
cream – 17 units (5382 holes)
ie each flower with its leaves and stalk needs four units of wool to cover 1018 holes.

Latchet hook

Extra cream rug wool in a skein, not cut, for binding the edges of the finished rug.

Very large blunt needle (knitter's needle, large-eyed tapestry needle) for binding and working.

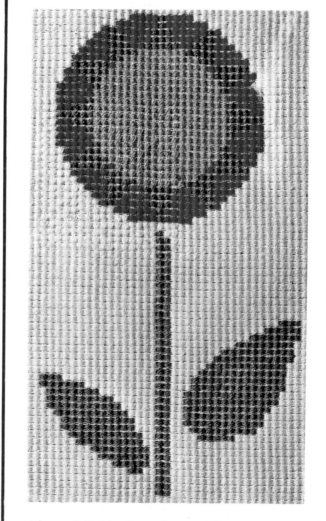

Above *Color plan for sunflower motif*
Left *Chart for rug – 1 square = 1 knot*

Preparing the edges

Fold a 1½ inches turning to the right side of the canvas on one of the raw edges, matching the holes and threads exactly with those of the canvas below. The outer rows of knots can then be made through the two layers of this fold.

To bind the turned edge, lay a strand of hank wool along it and overcast, using one of the methods shown on Page 13. Overcast the opposite raw edge roughly to prevent fraying; the hem at this edge should be turned as the square nears completion and overcast neatly as before.

To cover the canvas at the outer selvages, work a row of plait stitch one thread deep along the edges.

Working the design

To obtain an even finish, work horizontal rows using the four movement method of hooking (Page 11) across the canvas from left to right (or right to left if left-handed), from selvage to selvage beginning in the lower left-hand corner.

Above *Ideas for using the sunflower motif in a circular rug (left) or large rectangular rug (right)*

Panel by panel— a Japanese rug

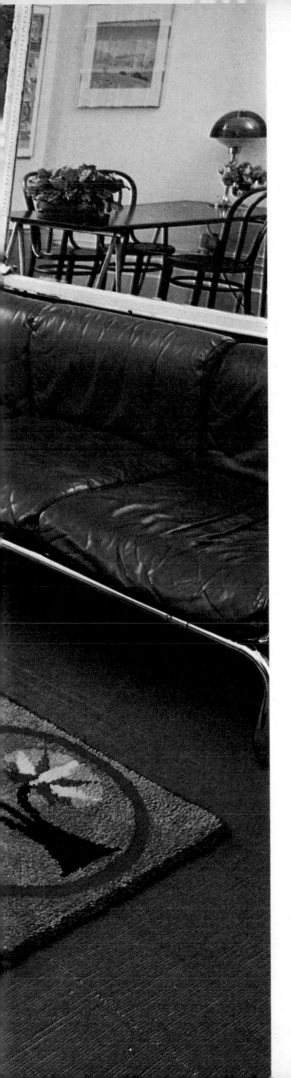

One of the easiest and most rewarding ways of rugmaking is to make up separate panels and then sew them together. Each of the panels on the superb and unusual hooked rug illustrated represents a Japanese family crest which was used originally to decorate the costume worn by a courtier on formal occasions and takes in many different aspects of Japanese life.

Experiment with color schemes
Each of the panels illustrated has been made up in a different color scheme to show the beautiful range of rug wools available but, by choosing your main color scheme, the rug can be made to fit in with any room. Another idea is to combine just two or three favorite motifs or even to work alternate squares plain. The possibilities are endless, and with some experimentation, the rug can be made to fit in with most decors. On completion the eight separate panels are simply sewn together in the desired order.

Measurements and yarn quantities
Each panel measures 2 feet square and the whole rug laid out as illustrated measures 48 inches by 96 inches. Each panel uses approximately 22 precut packs of rug wool. The amount of wool required for the eight-panel rug is therefore approximately 176 precut packs. In addition to this is the hank wool required for the binding and sewing together.

The crane

Materials required
Rug wool, precut in packs of 320 pieces, in the following colors and quantities: 14 packs mid royal; 2 packs each of scarlet, marigold and dark rose; 1 pack orange.

2 2 ounce hanks dark rose for binding.

0·7m ($\frac{3}{4}$ yard) rug canvas, approximately 10 holes to 3 inches, 24 inches wide.

Latchet hook

Very large blunt needle (knitter's needle, large-eyed tapestry needle or curved rug needle) for binding and finishing.

Preparing the edges
Fold a $1\frac{1}{2}$ inches turning to the right side of the canvas on one of the raw edges, matching the holes and threads of the turning exactly with those of the canvas below. The outer rows of knots can then be made through the two layers of this fold to give a firmer edge. The raw edges will be lost in the pile of the rug.
To bind the turned edge, lay a strand

Below *The colors of the rug can be adapted to fit in with any room scheme.*

of hank wool along it and overcast using one of the methods shown on Page 13. Overcast the opposite raw edge roughly to prevent fraying; the hem at this edge should be turned as the panel nears completion and overcast neatly as before. It is possible to save on the quantity of hank wool used to overcast the turned top and bottom edges of one panel until it is ready to be joined to the adjacent panel. The edges can then be joined by overcasting across the two panels at once.

To cover the canvas at the outer selvage, work a row of plait stitch one thread deep along the edge. The inner selvage need not be bound as it will be hidden when the rug is finished.

Working the design
The chart indicates the main motif and also the border. Each square on the chart represents one knot.

To obtain an even finish, work in horizontal rows across the canvas using the 4-movement method (Page 11) from selvage to selvage from left to right (or vice-versa if left-handed), beginning in the lower left-hand corner.

Three fans

Materials required
Rug wool, precut in packs of 320 pieces, in the following colors and quantities: 11 packs shire green; 3 packs kingfisher; 2 packs each of blue haze, helio and plum; 1 pack dark rose.

2 2 ounce hanks dark rose for binding.

$\frac{3}{4}$ yard rug canvas, approximately 10 holes to 3 inches, 24 inches wide.

Latchet hook.

Very large blunt needle (knitter's needle, large-eyed tapestry needle or curved rug needle) for binding and finishing.

Working the design
Prepare the edges as for The Crane and work pattern using 4-movement method (Page 11), working in horizontal rows across the canvas from selvage to selvage from left to right (or vice-versa if left-handed), beginning in the lower left-hand corner.

Whirlpool

Materials required

Rug wool, precut in packs of 320 pieces, in the following colors and quantities: 11 packs wedgewood; 3 packs each of mid royal, light blue and cream; 1 pack dark rose.

2 2 ounce hanks dark rose for binding.

¾ yard rug canvas, approximately 10 holes to 3 inches, 24 inches wide.

Latchet hook.

Very large blunt needle (knitter's needle, large-eyed tapestry needle or curved rug needle) for binding and finishing.

Working the design

Prepare the edges as for The Crane and work pattern using 4-movement method (Page 11), working in horizontal rows across the canvas from selvage to selvage from left to right (or vice-versa if left-handed), beginning in the lower left-hand corner.

Rising sun

Materials required

Rug wool, precut in packs of 320 pieces, in the following colors and quantities: 14 packs light green; 4 packs scarlet; 1 pack each of dark brown, light brown, beige and dark rose.

2 2 ounce hanks dark rose for binding.

¾ yard rug canvas, approximately 10 holes to 3 inches, 24 inches wide.

Latchet hook

Very large blunt needle (knitter's needle, large-eyed tapestry needle or curved rug needle) for binding and finishing.

Working the design

Prepare the edges as for The Crane and work pattern using 4-movement method (Page 11), working in horizontal rows across the canvas from selvage to selvage from left to right (or vice-versa if left-handed), beginning in the lower left-hand corner.

one small square represents one knot

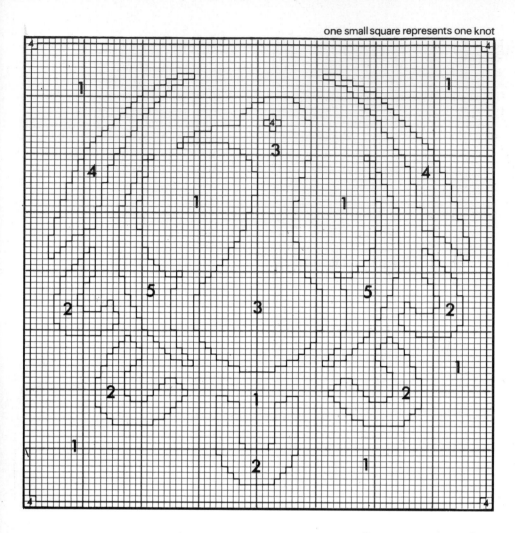

Chart for crane motif

Heavy rug wool

1 Mid-royal

2 Scarlet

3 Marigold

4 Dark rose

5 Orange

one small square represents one knot

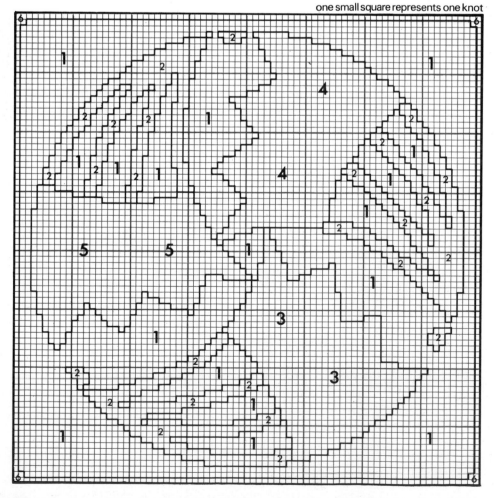

Chart for three fans motif

Heavy rug wool

1 Green

2 Kingfisher blue

3 Plum

4 Helio

5 Blue haze

6 Dark rose

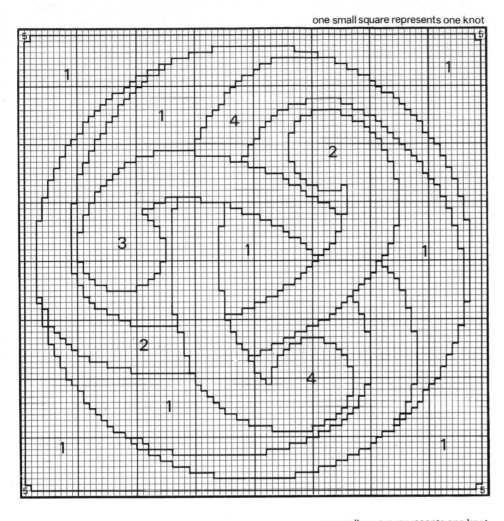

Chart for whirlpool motif

Heavy rug wool

1 Wedgcwood

2 Mid-royal

3 Light blue

4 Cream

5 Dark rose

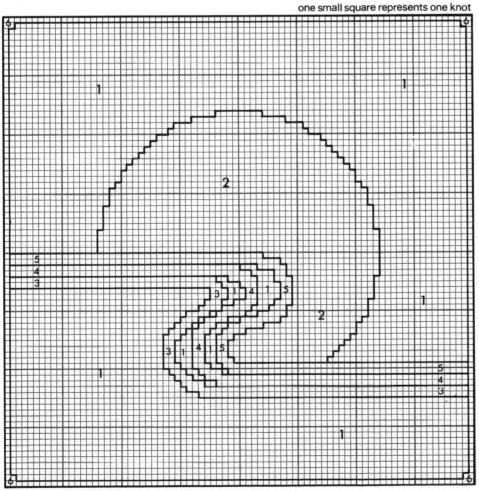

Chart for rising sun motif

Heavy rug wool

1 Light green

2 Scarlet

3 Dark brown

4 Light brown

5 Beige

6 Dark rose

Two fans

Materials required

Rug wool, precut in packs of 320 pieces, in the following quantities: 12 packs brush green; 5 packs pink; 2 packs plum: one pack each raspberry and dark rose.

2 2 ounce hanks dark rose for binding,

¾ yard rug canvas, approximately 10 holes to 3 inches, 24 inches wide.

Latchet hook

Very large blunt needle (knitter's needle, large-eyed tapestry needle or curved rug needle) for binding and finishing.

Working the design

Prepare the edges as for The Crane and work pattern using 4-movement method (Page 11), working in horizontal rows across the canvas from selvage to selvage from left to right (or vice-versa if left-handed), beginning in the lower left-hand corner.

Diamond flower

Materials required

Rug wool, precut in packs of 320 pieces, in the following colors and quantities: 11 packs wedgewood; 3 packs each peacock and blue haze; 2 packs each brick dust and beige; 1 pack dark rose.

2 2 ounce hanks dark rose for binding.

¾ yard rug canvas, approximately 10 holes to 3 inches, 24 inches wide.

Latchet hook

Very large blunt needle (knitter's needle, large-eyed tapestry needle or curved rug needle) for binding and finishing.

Working the design

Prepare the edges as for The Crane and work pattern using 4-movement method (Page 11), working in horizontal rows across the canvas from selvage to selvage from left to right (or vice-versa if left-handed), beginning in the lower left-hand corner.

Tea plant fruit

Materials required

Rug wool, precut in packs of 320 pieces, in the following colors and quantities: 8 packs each sage and brush green; 3 packs scarlet; 2 packs dark rose; 1 pack pink.

2 2 ounce hanks dark rose for binding.

¾ yard rug canvas, approximately 10 holes to 3 inches, 24 inches wide.

Latchet hook

Very large blunt needle (knitter's needle, large-eyed tapestry needle or curved rug needle) for binding and finishing.

Working the design

Prepare the edges as for The Crane and work pattern using 4-movement method (Page 11), working in horizontal rows across the canvas from selvage to selvage from left to right (or vice-versa if left-handed), beginning in the lower left-hand corner.

Hollyhock

Materials required

Rug wool, precut in packs of 320 pieces, in the following colors and quantities: 12 packs mid-royal; 3 packs brick dust; 2 packs each gold and mimosa; 1 pack each maroon, olive and dark rose.

2 2 ounce hanks dark rose for binding.

¾ yard rug canvas, approximately 10 holes to 3 inches, 24 inches wide.

Latchet hook

Very large blunt needle (knitter's needle, large-eyed tapestry needle or curved rug needle) for binding and finishing.

Working the design

Prepare the edges as for The Crane and work pattern using the 4-movement method (Page 11), working in horizontal rows across the canvas from selvage to selvage from left to right (or vice-versa if left-handed), beginning in the lower left-hand corner.

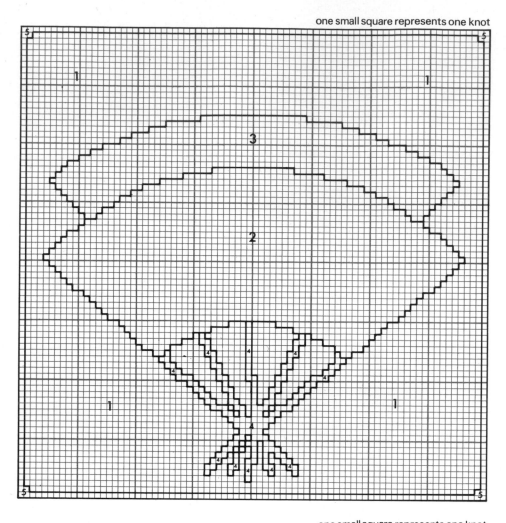

one small square represents one knot

Chart for two fans motif

Heavy rug wool

1 Brush Green

2 Pink

3 Plum

4 Raspberry

5 Dark rose

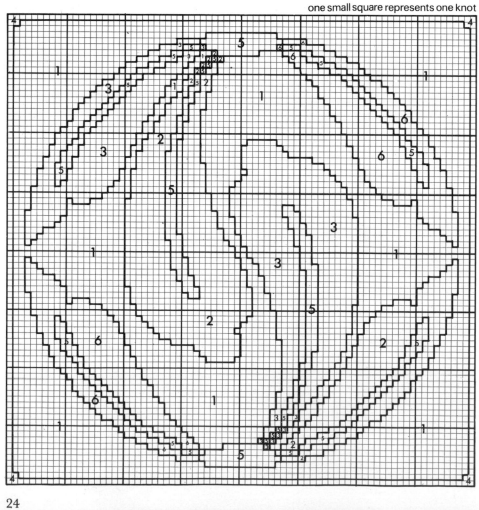

one small square represents one knot

Chart for diamond
flower motif

Heavy rug wool

1 Wedgewood

2 Peacock

3 Blue haze

4 Dark rose

5 Brick

6 Beige

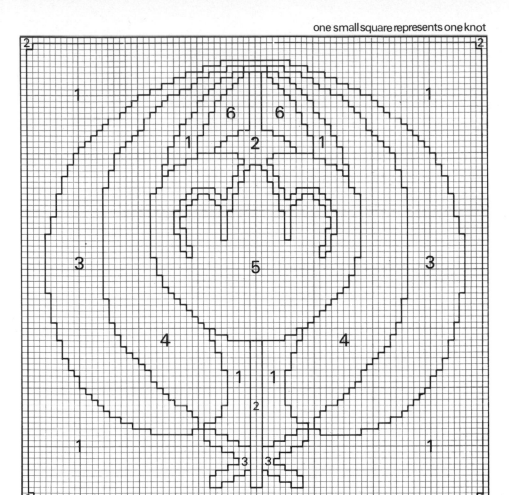

Chart for tea plant fruit motif

Heavy rug wool

1 Shire green

2 Dark rose

3 Sage

4 Brush green

5 Scarlet

6 Pink

Chart for hollyhock motif

Heavy rug wool

1 Mid-royal

2 Maroon

3 Gold

4 Olive

5 Brick

6 Mimosa

7 Dark rose

Sun motif floor cushion

The latchet hook method of rug making can also be used to make attractive and hard wearing cushions which are ideal for using on the floor.

The pile can be worked on both sides of the cushion or, if you prefer, you could make the back of the cushion from fabric. If you choose to work the pile on both sides, choose a darker color for the underside. However, if you decide to back the cushion with fabric, choose a backing that will stand up to some heavy wear and tear.

Materials required

For a cushion 36 inches square you will need: Canvas 39 inches by 36 inches, 1 hole per 3 inches

Rug yarn (320 pieces per pack); 12 cut packs green; 10 cut packs yellow; 7 cut packs orange; 18 cut packs off-white

Latchet hook

Backing fabric for cushion 39 inches square, such as burlap or velvet.

Matching sewing thread, needle

Felt-tipped pens in colors to match the yarns.

Cushion pad, 36 inches square

Starting and finishing

Because the raw edges of the canvas are enclosed inside the finished cushion, you can leave an unworked margin of canvas for 1 inch all the way round and use for your turnings when you make up the cushion.

Alternatively, if the size of the cushion corresponds to the width of canvas available, work the knots up to the selvages and use the selvages as a narrow turning. Allow 1 inch at each raw edge for turnings because the canvas may fray.

The design

Enlarge the design to scale and mark in the colors. Center the rug canvas over the design and trace the shapes of the areas onto it in the appropriate colors. Leave the blank canvas at each edge for the turnings.

Working the rug

Start working the rug using the 4-movement method (Page 11) from left

Left *The simple sun motif makes a luxurious indoor or outdoor floor cushion. You can choose a color for the border to tie in with your color scheme, but choose a durable backing material.*

Above *Working the rug. It is always wise to trace the complete pattern onto the rug canvas before starting to work the rug to prevent later mistakes.*
Right *Graph pattern for the simple sun motif. One square on the grid equals 3 inches.*

to right and keep working in parallel rows (right to left if you are left handed). Don't be tempted to do patches of the pattern and then fill up the canvas as this will give a very uneven finished appearance and, also with the thick wool, it is easy to miss squares.

Making up the cushion

Stitch back of the cushion to the canvas with right sides facing, by machining with a piping foot along the line of canvas nearest the first and last rows of knots and along the inside edge of one of the selvages. Leave the remaining side open.

Trim the raw edges to within $\frac{1}{2}$ inch of the stitching. Do not trim the selvages.

Turn the cushion over right side out and press the seams with your fingers.

Insert the cushion pad, fold under the turnings along the open side and slip-stitch firmly.

Hooked Oriental rug

Rugs based on Oriental designs are extremely attractive but exceedingly difficult to work. However, by simplifying and stylizing the basic design, a similar rug can be made using a latchet hook and cut rug yarn as for other short pile hooked rugs.

Materials required

To make a rug measuring 36 inches by 70 inches you will need: length of canvas, 2 yards by 36 inches, 10 holes per 3 inches.

Cut packs rug yarn: 38 packs mid-blue; 24 packs each antique gold and dark blue; 4 packs sun yellow and 2 packs primrose yellow.

2 skeins background color for edging

Latchet hook

Using the chart

The chart shows one complete quarter of the basic pattern plus the corner of the border. Trace the pattern onto the

rug from the chart before starting.

Fold a 1 inch turning to the right side of the canvas on one of the raw edges matching the holes and threads of the turning exactly with those of the canvas below. The outer rows of knots can then be worked through the two layers of this fold to give a firmer edge.

To bind the turned edge, lay a strand of hank wool along it and overcast using one of the methods shown on Page 13. Overcast the opposite raw edge roughly to prevent fraying; the hem at this edge should be turned as the panel nears completion and overcast neatly.

On the outer selvages, work a row of plain stitch one thread deep along the edge.

Working the design

Start working the rug using the 4-movement method (Page 11) from left to

right and keep working in parallel rows. Do not be tempted to do patches of the pattern and then fill up the canvas 'as this will give a very uneven finished appearance and, also with the thick wool, it is easy to miss squares.

Left *Chart for working the rug showing one complete quarter of the basic pattern and rug border.*
Right *Table showing the symbols for the working chart.*

Color	Symbol	No of cut packs
Primrose yellow		2
Antique gold		24
Sun yellow		4
Dark blue		24
Mid blue		38

Big bold lion rug for the playroom

Made in four separate sections, this colorful design can be used for cushions, wall hangings or makes a perfect rug for nursery or playroom. It is quite simple to make using the pattern shown on Page 32.

How to work and adapt the chart

If you are working from a chart, it makes it easier if the design is marked on the canvas with a felt pen first, marking color changes with a corresponding felt pen. Start by marking the lions' right legs, each six holes from the bottom of the canvas. By working carefully before starting to hook the rug mistakes can be avoided later.

Once the basic idea of the pattern has been grasped, you can alter it to fit your own canvas. Each lion takes 6400 holes and 23 units. Work out the total number of holes in the canvas (width holes multiplied by length holes) and subtract from it the number for each lion or lions. The resulting background number, divided by 320 will give you the number of wool units you will need in the background color.

Materials required

Each separate square on this rug as shown here is about 2 feet by 2 feet. Allowing for $1\frac{1}{2}$ inches at each end to turn under, you will need canvas 2 feet wide by 27 inches, you will need:

Yarn: total 6400 holes (80 x 80)

Col. A (main body and head)	5 units
Col. B (Tail, feet, mane)	5 units
Col. C (Highlights)	1 unit
Col. D (Features)	1 unit
Col. E (Background)	11 units

Latchet hook

Extra wool in a skein for binding the edges of the finished rug.

Very large blunt needle (knitter's needle, large-eyed tapestry needle or curved rug needle) for binding and finishing.

Working the edges

Lay your canvas on a table with the full length stretching away from you. To prevent the ends from fraying, fold the end of the canvas over for $1\frac{1}{2}$ inches, frayed ends uppermost, exactly matching each hole with the hole beneath. Tack, then work the first few rows of knots through this double thickness, so losing the rough ends in the pile of the rug.

Finish with an overcasting stitch (Page 13). If, however, the rug is to be made up of more than one panel it is possible to save on the quantity of hank wool used to overcast the top and bottom turned edges of one panel until it is ready to be joined to the adjacent panel. The edges can then be joined by overcasting across the two panels at once.

Working the rug

Start working the rug using the 4-movement method (Page 11) from left to right (right to left if you are left-handed) and keep working in parallel rows. Don't be tempted to do patches of the pattern and then fill up the canvas as this will give a very uneven finished appearance and, also, with the thick wool, it is easy to miss squares.

Make each of the individual squares following the diagram. Each little square stands for one knot. Remember, if you are making the four square rug, that the lion will have to be reversed on two of them so that the lions' heads will point inward.

To complete the rug

If you are making the rug of more than two panels and have joined them at the turned edges, you will have two long strips to be joined together.

The outer selvage should be completed by a plait stitch (Page 13). However do not overcast the inner selvage as this will be hidden when the rug is completed.

All that is necessary now is for the two strips to be joined down the center along the inner selvage. To do this, lay the panels flat, pile down, and pin the selvages together to form a plain seam. Using linen carpet thread double, sew along the base of the selvages with a firm backing stitch and press turnings flat.

Chart for big bold lion rug

A ■ B ■ C □ D ■

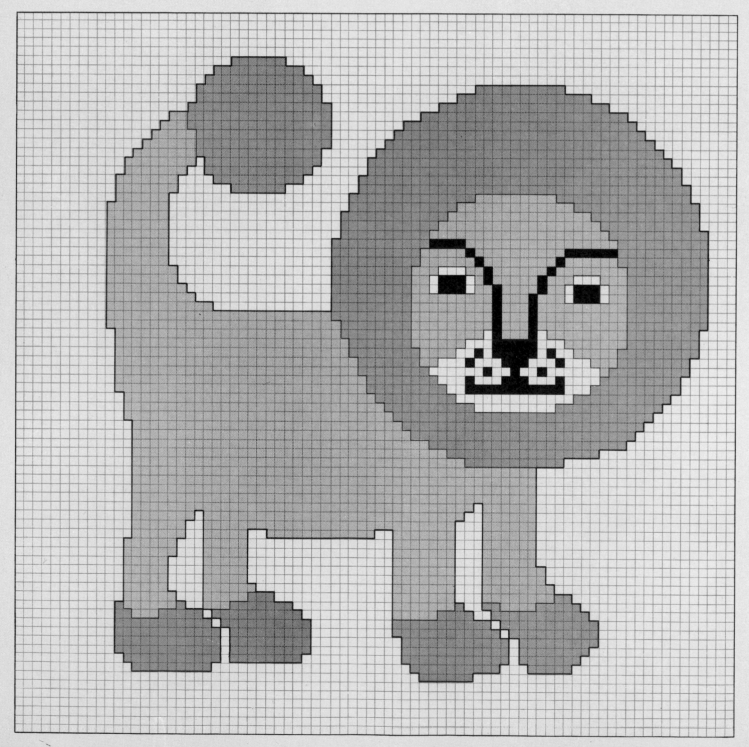

Long pile or rya rugs

Above *An attractive addition for the floor or the wall, a warm and cozy ray rug*

Rya means shaggy. Because the density of its pile is good insulation against the cold winters, the rya is found all over Scandinavia. Originally ryas were woven on a loom with the pile knotted on the warp threads by hand but now you can use a canvas foundation and knot the wool with a latchet hook.

Rya rugs have an individual style of coloring. Each knot is made of three strands of wool which allows enormous scope for using different shades of colour to build up a rich texture.

Materials

The canvas to use has 10 squares to 3 inches, and remember to buy enough to leave a $1\frac{1}{2}$ inches hem at each end. The most suitable wool is a twisted 2 ply coarse rug wool which comes in 1 ounce skeins (4 skeins to a hank). Each skein makes approximately 56 knots. A latchet hook is also required.

Cutting the skeins

Wool for rya rugs can be bought in pre-cut pieces but if you wish to you can cut your own. To do this, unravel the skein of wool and, holding it fully extended, cut cleanly through the two ends. Then fold these lengths in half and cut again, halve and cut once more. The skein is now divided into eight and you have a pile of cut threads. (It's a good idea to keep the different colored cut wools in separate polythene bags.) If the cut lengths seem a bit irregular don't bother to trim them as the general look of the rug is shaggy.

Working a rya

Turn in the rough ends as for the short pile rugs and work an edging stitch (Page 13) along one edge and partly up each selvaged edge.

Start to hook using the 4-movement method (Page 11) in the tufts from left to right (right to left if you are left-handed) using three strands of wool in each knot. With skeins of closely related colors, rather than complete contrasts, you can grade the colors as you wish, increasing or decreasing a color to get the required intensity or softness. Hook every alternate row; that is, leave one horizontal thread of canvas free between each row of knots.

Designing a rya rug

Rya rugs, as with short pile rugs, are available as canvases with already printed designs, so that you can choose your own colors, or you can buy a complete design in kit form which includes all the yarn. However, if you prefer to design your own rug, it is advisable to plan it on paper first so that you can estimate the amount of yarn you will need.

Aim at designs with curving bands of color, splashes of color in contrasting background, irregular stripes and, for more modern designs, geometric patterns. These are all far more effective than pictorial or flower designs which, as the long pile blurs the definition of the outlines, are not usually successful.

With modern, commercially dyed yarns you can introduce interesting color effects simply by using strands of different shades of one color, or even two or three different colors, in each knot. Related colors such as gray and pale blue, beige and pale pink, red and orange or yellow and green are usually the most successful combinations, but complementary colors used together in small areas can produce dramatic and unusual effects.

The additional advantage of blending is that if you do run out of a color before the rug is finished and have to buy more from a different dye lot, the color variation will be unnoticeable. Even on a monochrome rug, you could use two strands of one dye lot with one strand of another in each knot and any difference would be hidden.

Floor cushion

A rya floor cushion is quick to make and, as an introduction to the techniques, gives a good idea of the versatility of this method of rug making. The cushion can be made in any size – about 24 inches square makes a comfortable seat and is not too big to move about easily.

Working the rug

Having chosen the color blends for your design and estimated the amount of yarn needed, work the rug using the 4-movement method (Page 11) with three strands of wool in each knot. There is no necessity to work an edging stitch as you will be sewing it to a backing but leave the first and last threads free along the turned in ends.

When complete the cushion will need backing with a sturdy matching upholstery material as this is the side that will be getting the most wear.

Cut a square of backing material ¾ inch larger than the size of the worked canvas. Put the two right sides

together, pinning them firmly. Stitch through from the canvas side. On the selvages stab stitch through to the backing, catching each thread of canvas inside the selvage. Hem the other two edges catching the outside thread of each hole.

Leave one side open, turn inside out and stuff the cushion with either two old pillows or a 24 inch cushion pad.

Below left *The completed cushion worked in contrasting shades of blue and purple.*
Below right *Working the knots on rya rug canvas.*
Bottom right *Rya rugs are usually worked with strands of three different colors. Some of these blends are shown here, using brown as the basic color.*
Bottom *Working chart for the diamond patterned rya rug.*

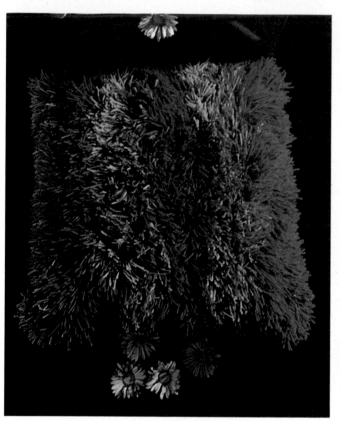

Top

Planning the design for a diamond-patterned rug. The knots are drawn in so that they can be counted easily to give the amount of yarn required.

Diamond pattern rug for beginners

A diamond pattern rug is an ideal first project as it gives the opportunity to experiment with various color schemes.

Drafting the design

Decide on the size of rug required and then divide it into diamonds. To do this, use graph paper which is printed with 10 squares to a unit so that each unit will correspond to 3 inches of canvas. Draw the shape of your rug to scale onto the paper and then divide the shape into equal-sized squares or rhombi (depending on the shape of diamond you want), using the lines of the graph paper as a guide.

From the squares or rhombi, draw the diamonds so that the diagonals pass through the intersections of the horizontal and vertical lines (Fig 1). Mark the position of the knots on one diamond, placing them on the lines of the graph in horizontal rows.

Calculating the yarn quantity

Count the number of knots to be worked in each diamond; multiply by the number of diamonds to be worked in each color or combinations of color and multiply this by the number of strands in each color. From this you can calculate the number of cut strands in each color you require. Remember when buying canvas to allow 3 inches each unselvaged end for turnings.

Working the rug

Place the canvas on a table with the selvages to your left and right and with the full length away from you. To make a neat strong edge, turn up the cut edge nearest you along a single weft bar for about 3 inches with the holes matching the holes underneath. Baste down. Repeat along the opposite edge.

Work the long pile by knotting the strands of wool, three at a time, over the single bars of the canvas. One knot is worked in every double hole. Work the first row of knots from left to right on the single bar of canvas on the fold at the end nearest you, and work as for the 4-movement method (Page 11).

Continue to work the knots in this way following your guide to the colors on the chart. Complete each row before beginning the next so there is no danger of missing a square. Work the last row on the single bar along the fold at the opposite end.

Ripple rya rug

This up-to-the-minute rya rug would make a splendid addition to any room. The yarn quantities are specified for the colours used for the rug in the photograph but you can easily substitute colors of your own choice.

Materials required

To make the rug measuring 24 inches by 48 inches you will need:

Rya rug canvas 52 inches by 24 inches

Rya rug yarn (168 pieces per cut pack) see chart below

Graph paper or dressmaker's squared paper, 24 inches × 48 inches

Felt-tipped pens or paints, preferably in colors to correspond with the yarns

Working the rug

Enlarge the design to scale. Place the canvas over the design so that 2 inches extends at each end. Trace the design onto the canvas using the felt-tipped pens or paints to mark the outlines of the areas in the appropriate colors.

Place the canvas on a table with the selvages to your left and right and with the full length away from you. To make a neat strong edge, turn up the cut edge nearest you along a single weft bar for about 2 inches with the holes matching the holes underneath. Baste down. Repeat along the opposite end of the canvas.

Chart for ripple design rug

Color	No. packs	No. strands in each color per area					
		A	B	C	D	E	F
off-white	45	3				1	
light grey	16		2				
dark grey	15		1		2		
grey-blue	15			1		2	
caramel	10			1			1
tan	10			1			1
mid-brown	4						1
dark brown	4				1		
		3	3	3	3	3	3

Right *Graph pattern for ripple rug. Each square represents one hole in the canvas and the rows of knots are indicated by arrows at the side of the graph.*

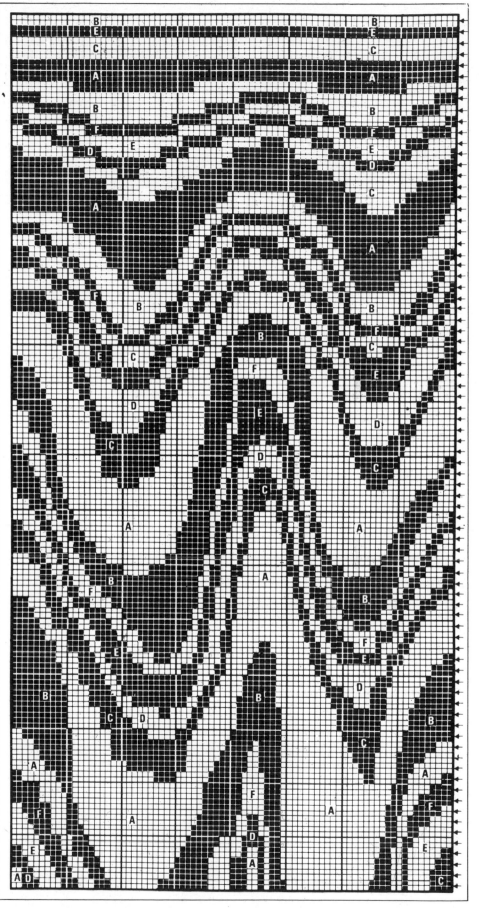

Work the long pile of the rug over single bars of the canvas, using the four movement method (Page 11).

Continue to work the knots following the guide to the colors given on the chart. Complete each row before beginning the next so there is no danger of missing a square. Work the last row on the single bar along the fold at the opposite end.

A bright color-blended rya rug

A warm and soft rya rug will always form a highlight of any room. The rug illustrated is used to add a bold splash of color to a light and airy bedroom.

Materials required
To make the rug measuring 27 inches by 54 inches including overhanging pile, you will need:

1½ yards Rya rug canvas with 10 squares to 3 inches, 24 inches wide. Alternatively, use Turkey rug canvas and work the knots on alternate rows.

Pre-cut rya yarn (168 strands per cut pack): 52 packs pale olive; 26 packs dark sea green; 2-3 packs pale yellow; 3 packs bright yellow; 12 packs gold.

Latchet hook

Tacking thread and needle.

Working the rug
Place the canvas on a table with the selvages to your left and right and with the full length away from you. To make a neat strong edge turn up the cut edge nearest you along a single weft bar for about 3 inches with the holes matching the holes underneath. Baste. Repeat along the opposite edge of the canvas.

The long pile of the rug is worked by knotting the strands of wool, three at a time, over the single bars of the canvas (Fig 1). One knot is worked in every double hole. Work the first row of knots from left to right on the single bar of canvas on the fold at the end nearest you, and work as for the 4-movement method.

Continue to work the knots in this way following the guide to the colors as given on the chart. Complete each row before beginning the next so there is no danger of missing a square. Work the last row on the single bar along the fold at the opposite end.

Below *Diagram of the color-blended rya rug showing the layout of the color sections. The pattern for this section is given overleaf.*

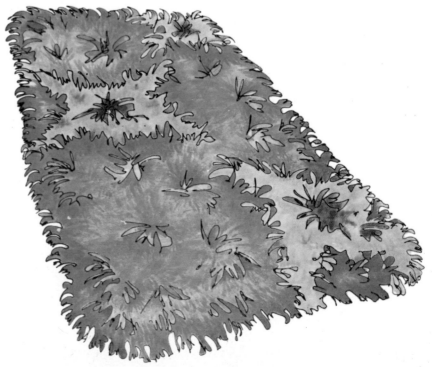

Color key

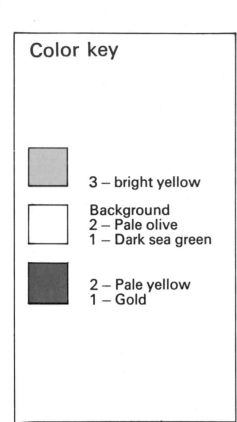

3 – bright yellow

Background
2 – Pale olive
1 – Dark sea green

2 – Pale yellow
1 – Gold

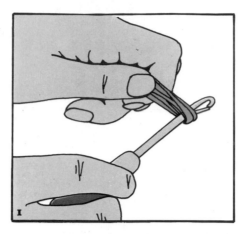

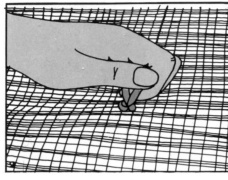

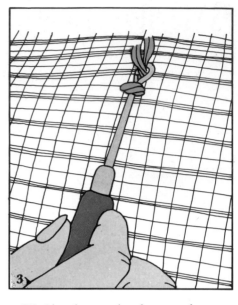

1 *Working the rug using three strands of yarn*
2 *Work each knot on the single bar of the rug canvas. Work one knot in every double hole.*
3 *Pulling the knot tight.*

Motif for rya rug

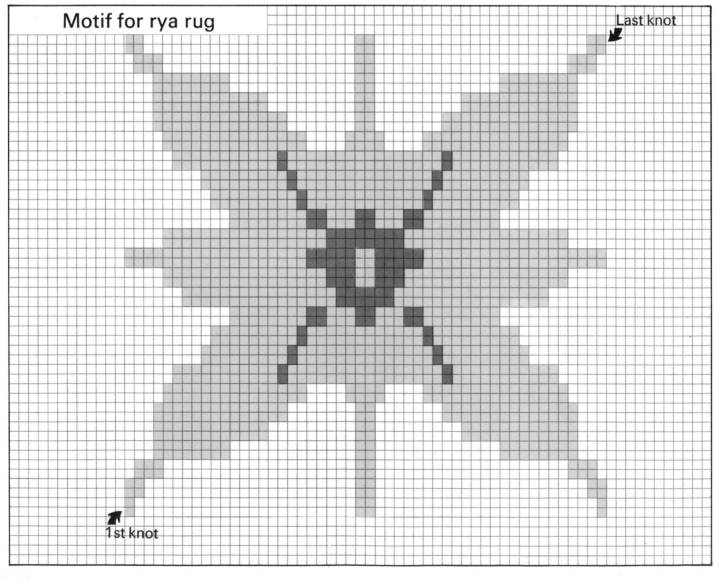

Last knot

1st knot

Stitchmade tapestry rugs

This method of making rugs using embroidery stitches is very familiar to other kinds of tapestry work. You can make cushions, stool tops and wall hangings in the same way, and which will suit any setting.

The design

With stitch-made rugs, you can either make a pile surface or a flat surface. Both wear well and take about the same time and skill to make, but a pile surface uses about 1 ounce more of wool per square foot on coarse canvases.

A pile rug is more traditional and, for some people more luxurious, but a smooth-surfaced rug gives more opportunity for variety because different stitches can be used and make it more interesting to work.

As with any other kind of tapestry work, you can buy kits consisting of canvas printed with designs, together with the right amount of wool. This is the easiest way if you want to make a rug with a traditional or complicated pattern, but it is also the most expensive.

Alternatively, you can buy a chart which shows the formation of the design, and adapt it proportionally to fit the size of the rug you want. This involves using squared graph paper – normally one quarter of the size of the rug, but full-size in the case of asymmetrical patterns – so you can work out precisely how the pattern will fall. This method gives you the chance of choosing your own colors, and also of saving money by buying the wool direct from carpet factories.

You should always be careful to buy enough wool in each color, because if you run out you may not be able to get the same color later. In fact, slight changes of color are characteristic of many valuable Oriental carpets, and in other types are often deliberately introduced to give variation to a large area, but this sort of thing is usually better planned in advance.

If you feel like designing your own rug, for your first attempts it is wisest to start with a very simple geometric pattern or perhaps adapt an existing one. Buy paper printed with small squares which correspond to the size of your canvas and use colored pencils to sketch in your design. Work out several roughs of the main pattern first before you design the whole rug.

Since carpets are normally seen from

Left *A stitchmade daisy rug.*
These rugs, worked completely in cross stitch, are both attractive and durable.

41

all directions, you will probably find that a strictly symmetrical design is the easiest type to start with, because you need design only a quarter of it. The pattern should be reversed on each of the remaining quarters.

In a room where you do not want a rug with a pattern, you can add interest to a plain one by combining different stitches, or by alternating pile and smooth-surfaced sections. Often you can add depth to a carpet by combining two shades of the same color, particularly in those cases where you are using two strands of wool in the needle together.

The size of the rug you make will obviously depend on where you will be putting it, but for rectangular rugs you will usually find that it is easiest to base the width on one of the standard widths available in the type of canvas you are using, and to make the length one and three-quarter times this size.

The wool

Only wool yarn should be used for rug making because it is hard-wearing, does not attract the dirt quickly, is available in the right sort of thickness and has an advantage over man-made yarns in that its hairy texture helps cover the foundation canvas.

The thickest type of wool available is 6-ply wool yarn. Carpets made with this are very strong, but also heavy and rather coarse. They are the quickest to make, but are also the most expensive because so much wool is needed.

For a finer carpet, you should use 2-ply carpet wool. This is quicker and coarser than 2-ply knitting wools, and is sold at needlework shops. It is often possible – and cheaper – to buy it in the form of thrums from a carpet factory. This is the leftover yarn which the factory cannot use. It tends to vary slightly in thickness, so you may have to use two strands instead of one in some cases.

Two-ply crewel wool, which is often used for other kinds of tapestry work, should not be used for carpets because it is too soft to withstand continual friction. If you do want a finer yarn than 2-ply carpet wool, it is better to use Brussels thrums because these are stronger. These are often supplied in loose twists of several strands, which should be separated before use.

The canvas

Rug canvas, which is the foundation on which the stitches are worked, is available by the yard in a variety of widths, and with 3, 4, 5, 6, 7, 8, 9 or 10 holes to 1 inch. It is essential that the correct

canvas is chosen for the type of wool being used, because if too thick a wool is used for the size of hole, the stitches will be difficult to work and will distort the shape of the finished rug, so that it will not lie flat. On the other hand, if you use too fine a wool, the rug will be floppy and the threads of the canvas will show through.

As a guide, 6-ply rug wool should be used only on canvas with three holes to 1 inch. On the intermediate sizes, with 4, 5 or 7 holes to 1 inch, it would be too thick but one strand of 2-ply is not enough, so here you should use two strands. On the finer canvases, use two or three strands of Brussels thrums.

Except on the very finest canvas, the mesh is formed by two threads each way which separate the holes into which the needle is inserted. Except in certain stitches, these threads should be counted as one, and the stitches worked over both. It is possible to buy single-mesh canvas which corresponds to the sizes above, but it is more difficult to use because the stitches have to be worked over two consequent threads, and it frays quickly.

Preparing the canvas

To prevent the canvas from fraying during working and to strengthen the edges when the rug is finished and in use, it is essential to prepare it correctly, and a minimum turning of 2 inches should be made by folding over this edge along a weft thread, so that the holes correspond with the holes underneath. The edge should be firmly overcast in position with matching sewing thread.

The opposite edge should be prepared in a similar way, although the sewing can be less neat here because you may have to adjust the width of the turning later to fit the pattern.

The selvages can be finished using one of the methods on Page 13 before you start the main stitching but it is usually safer to complete them afterwards. This is particularly so with smooth-surfaced rugs because the type of stitching used tends to pull the canvas out of shape and this is easier to correct if the edges have not been finished.

Starting off

Before you plunge into making a full-size rug, it is always worth working a sampler. This will give you a chance to try out the various stitches and wools and it will not matter if you have to unpick anything and distort the canvas in the process. If the sampler is a sucess, it may make a very attractive cushion or stool cover.

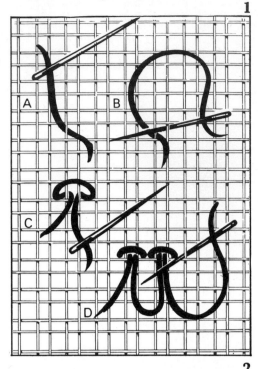

Below *Working Turkey knot stitch*

1

2

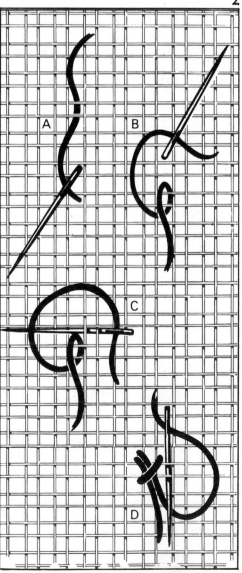

Above *Working Surrey stitch*

Above *A modern interpretation of a traditional design* **Below left** *A corner detail* **Below right** *Detail of back*

For pile rugs, the canvas should be arranged so that the folded edge is towards you, with the raw edge uppermost, the selvages on your left and right and the unworked length of canvas stretching away from you. Start working the stitches in the first hole from the fold on the left-hand edge (left-handed people may prefer to start at the right-hand edge). Work a complete row across the canvas, changing color where necessary.

Don't be tempted into working blocks of color instead of complete rows, because you may find that by doing so you miss holes or make other mistakes. To save time, however, and to avoid wasting lengths of wool, it is a good idea to have several needles threaded with the appropriate colors.

For smooth-surfaced rugs, arrange the canvas so that the folded end where you are starting work is away from you, with the cut edge on the underside and the unworked length towards you. The only exception to this rule is if you are using Soumak stitch (see below). With these types of rugs, you can generally work in blocks of color most efficiently, and this will save on the number of joins necessary.

Start off with a 18 inches to 24 inches length of wool in the needle. You will find that it will be used up quickly, particularly with a pile rug, but do not use longer lengths in order to avoid joins, because with the constant friction caused by pulling the wool in and out of the canvas, it will start to fray and may eventually break.

With pile stitches, the ends of each length form part of the pile on the front of the rug, and do not need any special methods of securing because the formation of the stitch is enough. With smooth-surfaced stitches, however, the end should be held on the underside of the canvas and caught in the stitches.

If you are using two lengths of wool in the needle, make sure that these lie flat side by side on the canvas, and are not twisted.

The stitches

One of two stitches can be used to make a carpet with a pile: Surrey stitch (Fig. 2), so named because it was devised by a member of the Surrey Women's Institute in England, and Turkey or Ghiordes stitch (Fig. 1) which is similar in formation to the knot used by Oriental workers.

The two stitches give a very similar appearance on the front of the carpet, but Surrey stitch is stronger and gives a neater finish to the back, although it does take longer to work.

The length of the pile made by either stitch is optional, but a length of $\frac{3}{4}$ inch on canvas with three or four holes to 1 inch is most satisfactory; a shorter pile should be used on finer canvases. There is no need to use a gauge or guide to keep the loops a consistent length because they can always be trimmed evenly later, and you will soon find that with practice you can make them the same size. Cut the loops after each row is worked.

The best stitches for smooth-surfaced carpets are those which are worked diagonally across the mesh of the canvas, because this helps ensure that the threads are completely covered. Variations of cross stitch are most commonly used, but many other traditional embroidery stitches are also good and interesting effects can be made by combining them. Other popular stitches are Soumak stitch and Gobelin stitch. (Figs. 3–4).

A rug made with Soumak stitch (Fig. 3) looks like a loom-woven Oriental Soumak rug. The method of working it is different from other stitch-made rugs in that the unworked canvas is held to your left-hand side with the selvage running sideways. Regardless of the direction in which you are working – from side to side, top to bottom or diagonally – the V made by each stitch should always have its point lying along the weft of the canvas and toward you.

The stitch is fairly tricky to work until you get the knack, because the point of the V is made by inserting the needle between the double weft threads and each stitch interlocks with those above and below. This makes unpicking difficult, although the resulting surface is very strong and does not use much wool.

Gobelin stitch is a much simpler interlocking stitch which is formed by working a row of stitches across the canvas from right to left, and then another row, which overlaps the first row, from left to right. It is a very quick stitch to work, but is best kept for plain or striped rugs because it does not work well for intricate designs (Fig. 4).

Finishing the rug

Most rugs need stretching to show them off to best advantage, and this is particularly important with smooth-surfaced ones which may have become

distorted.

The easiest place to do this is on a bare planked floor, where you can follow the lines of the boards as a guide. With its right side facing up, tack one long edge of the carpet to the floor, keeping the side completely flat, but without stretching it. The tacks need not be very close together at this stage. Then tack down one of the adjacent sides, making sure that it is at right angles. Pull the fourth corner so that the other long side is also at right angles to the short sides, and so that it is the same length as the opposite edge. Tack this down as well, then insert further tacks all around so that the carpet is completely surrounded by tacks about 1 inch apart.

Cover the rug with sheets of blotting paper and soak these thoroughly with cold water. Using a hot iron, press carefully all over, including the side edges. Leave the rug for a few days until it is completely dry.

Below *A hardwearing flat stitch rug made in a modern geometrical design*

Above *Detail of rug worked in Soumak stitch*

Below *Example of interlocking Gobelin stitch*

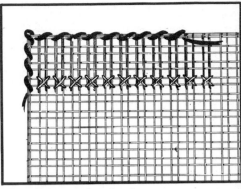

Above *Overcasting the edges*

Below *Vertical Soumak stitch*

3

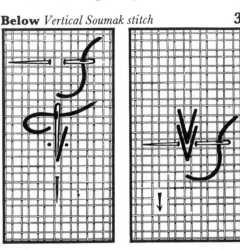

Below *Vertical and diagonal Soumak stitch*

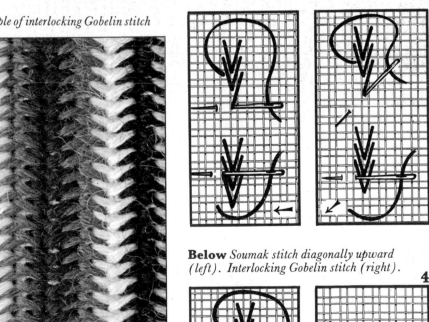

Below *Soumak stitch diagonally upward (left). Interlocking Gobelin stitch (right).*

4

Combining stitches— a textured rug

This quietly elegant, circular rug would make a perfect centerpiece for a living room or bedroom. The attractive texture is produced by working the flat areas in plain wool in cross stitch and the pile areas in two-tone wool in Surrey stitch.

Materials required
To make the finished rug measuring 48 inches diameter, including overhanging pile, you will need:

1⅜ yards rug canvas with approximately 10 squares to 3 inches and 48 inches wide.

22 x 2 ounces skeins rug wool, plain shade.

22 x 2 ounces skeins rug wool, two-tone shade.

Rug needle

4 yards carpet binding approximately 2 inches wide.

Linen carpet thread

Heavy needle

Colored pencil.

1 pr of embroidery scissors and dressmaking scissors

Preparing the canvas
Fold the canvas in half in both directions and mark the center thread with colored pencil.

Following the chart
The chart shows a quarter of the rug, with the center rows in both directions marked between the heavy double lines. Each square on the chart represents one stitch and the motif in the square shows the particular stitch to be used.

Working the stitches
Work the stitches along the center rows of the rug first, changing wool and stitching according to the chart.

Complete each quarter of the rug, working from the center out but without repeating the center rows. Work in rows for as many stitches as required in one color, then work the rows above in the same color, thus completing a whole block before moving on to the other color.

The cross stitch used in rugmaking is very similar to that used for embroidery. However, it can be varied according to the direction in which you are working. Ensure that the needle always goes in the same direction for each stitch otherwise a very uneven result will be achieved. For example, if the first stitch of the cross passes diagonally from left to right and the second stitch passes over this from left to right, then all the stitches should follow suit.

The instructions for Surrey stitch are given on page 42. Where, however, you are working a row of cross stitch above Surrey stitch, work the bottom of the cross stitches into the top holes of the Surrey stitch.

Finishing off
When all the stitches have been worked, trim the surplus canvas to within 1 inch of the stitches. Turn the canvas onto the back of the rug and press down. Pin the carpet braid over the raw edge and stitch the outer edge.

Make darts where necessary along the inner edge of the braid to make it lie flat and overcast in position.

The darts should be spaced as evenly as possible for a neat finish.

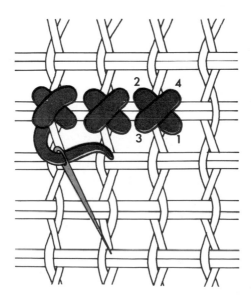

Above *Working simple cross stitch. The numbers demonstrate the way in which the stitch should be formed.*

Chart for textured rug

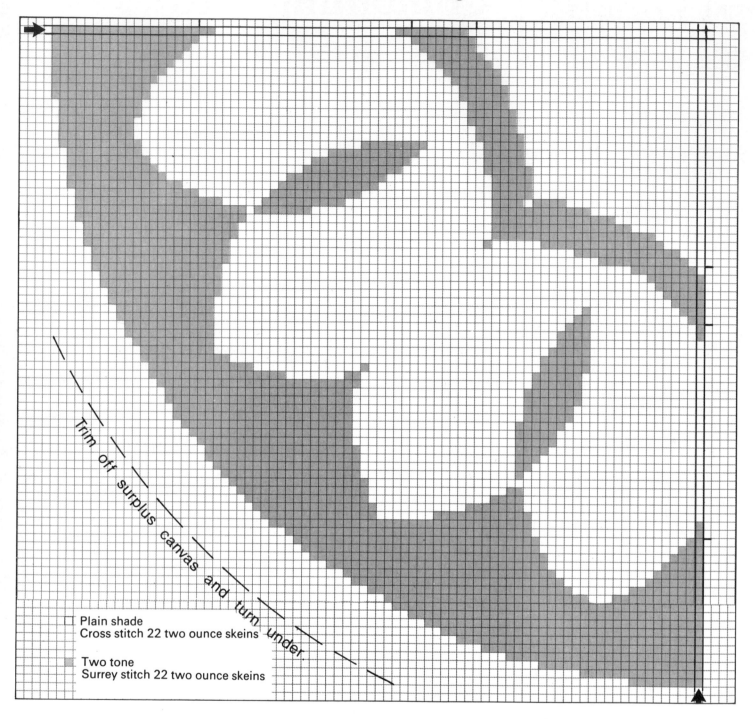

Trim off surplus canvas and turn under.

☐ Plain shade
Cross stitch 22 two ounce skeins

▨ Two tone
Surrey stitch 22 two ounce skeins

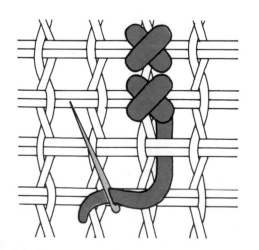

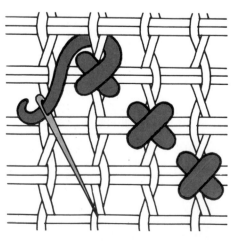

Left *Working cross stitch. The stitches can be made in any direction, vertically or horizontally, but for a really neat finish, it is best to insure that the second stitch always crosses the first in the same direction as the previous stitches.*

A garland of roses

This cross-stitched design of pink roses, syringa blossom and burnished autumn leaves looks beautiful whether worked as a rug or adapted to a cushion or a framed picture.

Materials required

¾ yard 36 inches wide rug canvas with 10 double threads to 1 inch.

Tapestry needle   size 14

Carpet thrums approximately 5 ounces for every square foot.

It is advisable to buy sufficient thrums at one time as colors are inclined to vary each time they are purchased from different dye lots.

Transferring the design

It is much easier if the design is marked on the canvas first. To do this find the center of the rug and working outwards, follow the pattern on page 00, transfering the design, using a felt tipped pen.

A complete quarter of the border is given on Page 50. Find the middle of the rug width and length at the border and match the pattern to this and the center of the rug. Mark the pattern.

It is often better to mark the complete pattern before starting to work the rug to avoid making mistakes later, although if you are good at following patterns a few strategic guidelines may be enough.

Work from the center of the design outward, making cross stitches over one double thread each way. Remember each square on the pattern represents one stitch.

The cross stitch used in rugmaking is very similar to that used for embroidery. However, it can be varied according to the direction in which you are working. Ensure that the needle always goes in the same direction for each stitch otherwise a very uneven result will be achieved. For example if the first stitch of the cross passes diagonally from left to right and the second stitch passes over this from left to right, then all the stitches should follow suit.

Above *The completed rug*

Finishing

When you have finished stitching the design, stretch the canvas (see page 44) and trim away excess fabric, leaving 1½ inches of canvas all around.

Overcast to prevent fraying and turn the 1½ inches edge under to the wrong side. Pin and tack the turned hem, finishing the rug with hem stitching all around in strong cotton.

Above *A cushion using only the center design*

Right *A classically elegant rug worked completely in simple cross stitch*

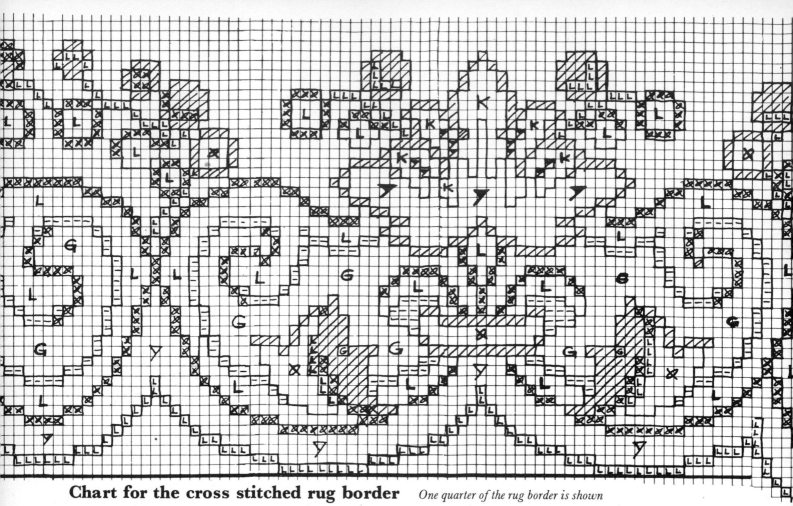

Chart for the cross stitched rug border   *One quarter of the rug border is shown*

The diagram shows how to fit the four quarters of the rug border together with the rug center design.

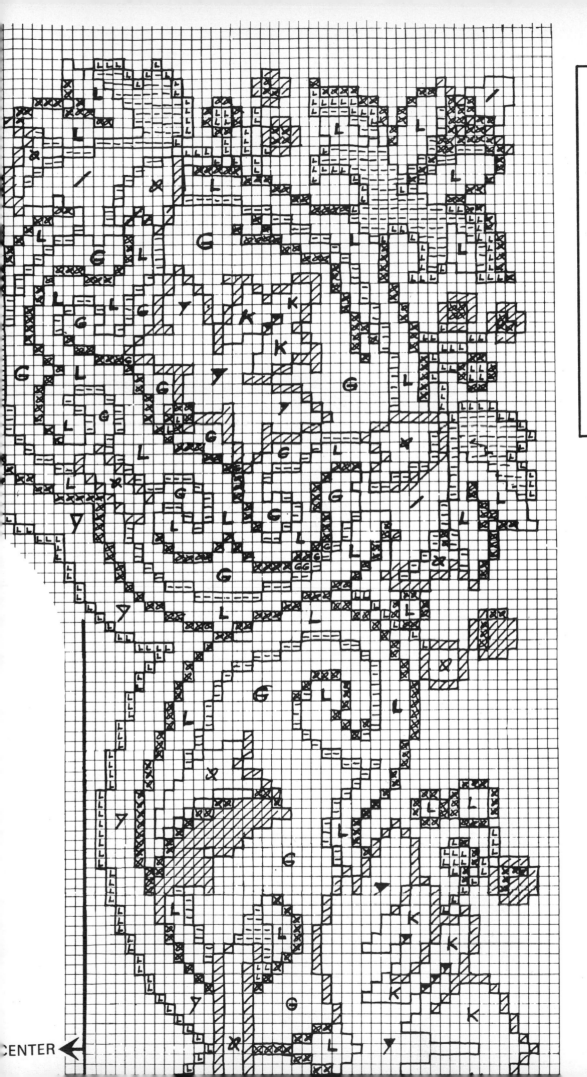

Color key for rug border

Each square = one cross-stitch. Yarn amounts appear in ( )

- ⧅ rust (6)
- ⊠ salmon pink (8)
- ⧄ light green (12)
- L light olive (24)
- G beige (24)
- K red (4)
- − deep beige (12)
- ⧄ pale pink (12)

Background to rug edge olive green

CENTER ⭠

Chart for the cross stitched rug

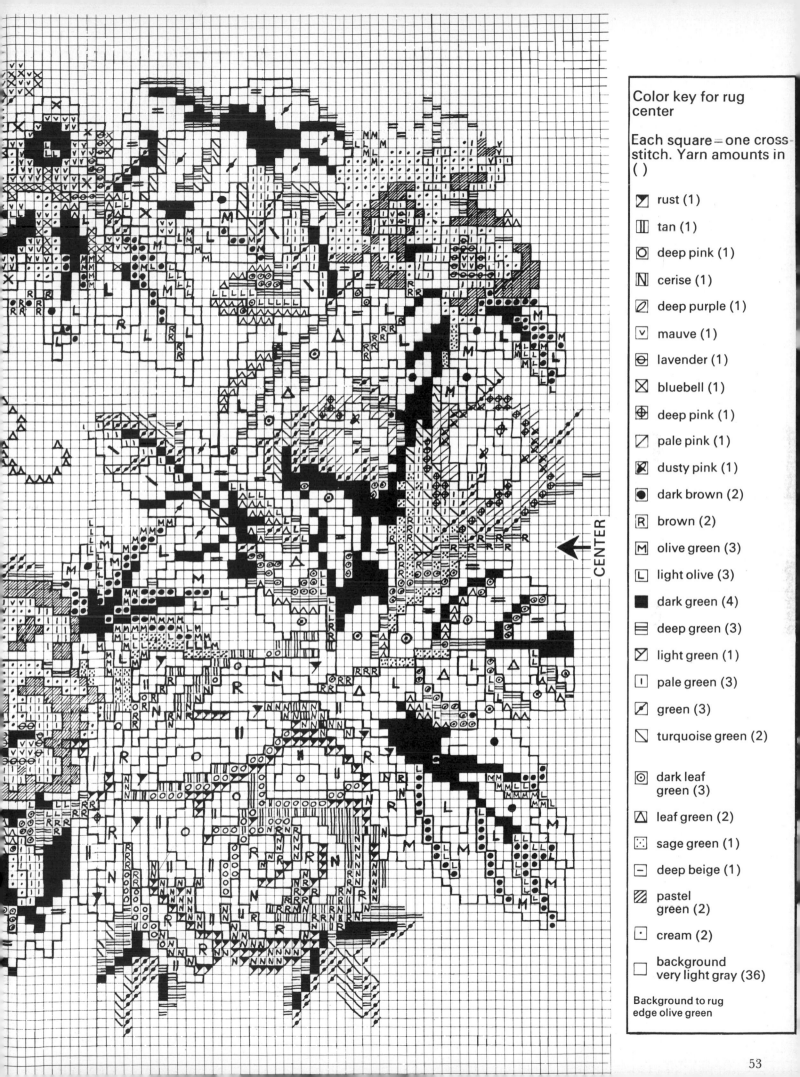

Color key for rug center

Each square = one cross-stitch. Yarn amounts in ( )

rust (1)

tan (1)

deep pink (1)

cerise (1)

deep purple (1)

mauve (1)

lavender (1)

bluebell (1)

deep pink (1)

pale pink (1)

dusty pink (1)

dark brown (2)

brown (2)

olive green (3)

light olive (3)

dark green (4)

deep green (3)

light green (1)

pale green (3)

green (3)

turquoise green (2)

dark leaf green (3)

leaf green (2)

sage green (1)

deep beige (1)

pastel green (2)

cream (2)

background very light gray (36)

Background to rug edge olive green

CENTER

Tibetan poppy

Stitch a bright Tibetan poppy to add color to your room or combine a whole garden of poppies in a squared design to form a handsome rug and make up one square to make a matching cushion.

Materials required

To make the rug of the finished measurement of 48½ inches by 32½ inches you will need:
Canvas about 4 squares to 1 inch 52 inches by 36 inches.
Rug wool. Number of 2 ounce hanks in brackets. 1. Turquoise (21). 2. mid-royal (23). 3. gorse gold (5) 4. light olive (33) 5. heath green (37).

Rug needle

Working the rug

Mark the center of the rug widthwise and work out the pattern on the canvas to avoid making mistakes later. For the first row work from the chart from the center outward to establish the center of the design remembering that 1 square on the pattern represents one stitch. From then on work across the complete row.

The cross stitch used in rugmaking is very similar to that used for embroidery. However, it can be varied according to the direction in which you are working. Ensure that the needle always goes in the same direction for each stitch otherwise a very uneven result will be achieved. For example if the first stitch of the cross passes diagonally from left to right and the second stitch passes over this from left to right, then all the stitches should follow suit.

Finishing

When you have finished stitching the design, stretch the canvas (see page 36) and trim away excess fabric, leaving approximately 1½ inches of canvas all around.

Overcast to prevent fraying and turn the edge under to the wrong side. Pin and tack the turned hem, finishing the rug with hem stitching all around in strong cotton.

Chart and color plan for one square

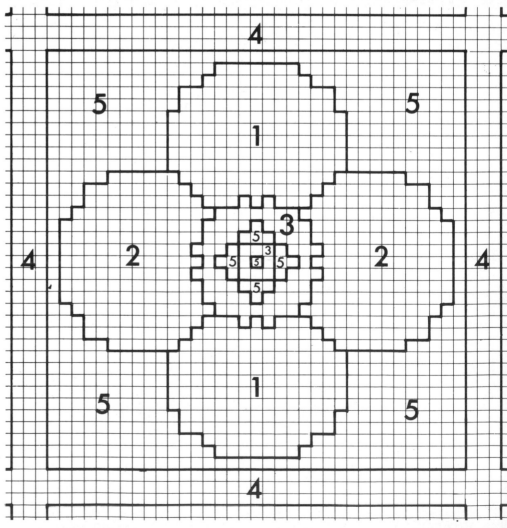

Spacecraft in stitches

The designer of this bold and brilliant rug for a boy's room has adapted a series of spacecraft shapes then worked the resulting design on rug canvas. Areas of cross stitch combine with tufted shapes – all in good, strong colors – to create a unique composition of texture and relief.

Materials required to make the rug:
To make the rug measuring 24 inches by 39 inches, excluding fringe you will need:
1¼ yards 24 inches rug canvas, marked in 3 inch squares (in order to have canvas correspond with diagram for working, allow at least one half of a 3 inches square at either end of this yardage).

Latchet hook

Very large blunt needle.

Rug tufts (precut in bundles of 320) in the following colors and quantities:
Rust – 9 bundles
Mauve – 7 bundles
Orange – 4 bundles

Knitting worsted (2 ounce balls) for the cross stitch areas in the following colors and quantities:
Black – 5 balls including 2 balls for fringe.
Dark purple – 2 balls
Plum – 3 balls
Cream – 1 ball

To make the rug
Measure 39 inches from one colored guideline to another, lengthwise on the canvas. Allow an extra six threads beyond this line at each end for the turnings, and cut the canvas at this point. Fold this extra canvas back along the double thread beyond the last colored line at each end, matching up all the holes; this allows one extra row to work the fringe. Baste the turnings under.

Following the stitch chart, work the outlines in black cross stitch, using a double strand of knitting wool in the large needle. Each square represents one cross stitch and the heavy grid corresponds exactly to the colored lines woven into the canvas. Thus it is quite simple to cross-check the design.

Make the edging along the top and bottom selvages in buttonhole stitch, using a single strand of black knitting

Below *One corner of the canvas being worked reveals stitches, edging and fringe.*

wool and working three stitches in each hole of the canvas.

Filling the design

Chart 2 indicates which areas are worked in cross stitch and which in tufts. The key for this chart also gives the color of each shape.

The tufts are worked over the straight double threads of the canvas and can face in either direction as long as all are in the same direction.

Work the small window shapes in orange tufts before working the surrounding area.

Work the cross stitches vertically, from the top to the bottom of the design, using a double strand of knitting wool. This will give a plait-like effect. To work horizontal lines in the design, turn the canvas on its side and work in the same way. Areas of cross stitch should be worked from the right-hand side of a shape to the left, finishing off each row at the end and starting a new one at the top.

Allow about $1\frac{1}{2}$ inches of wool on the wrong side of the canvas before beginning to stitch; this loose end is then caught in with the first few stitches. Finish off by threading about the same amount of wool through the line of stitches on the wrong side.

Making the fringe

Cut 9 inch lengths of the black knitting wool by winding it over a piece of cardboard $4\frac{1}{2}$ inches wide, then cutting through it once. Use a double strand of wool for each knot: Fold in half and pull the loop from the wrong side, so that each loop shows when the fringe is pulled through. Work the fringe at either end of the rug – no finishing off is required as the rough edges of the canvas have already been folded to the wrong side and worked during the making of the rug.

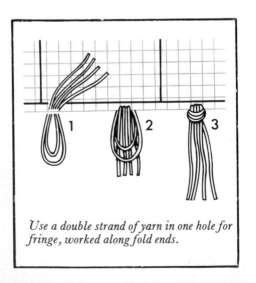

Use a double strand of yarn in one hole for fringe, worked along fold ends.

Key to color areas

Color	Stitch	Shape Number
Rust	Tufts	1, 4, 7, 10, 13, 18, 24
Mauve	Tufts	2, 6, 12
Orange	Tufts	9, 15a-b, 16a-b, 21, 25, 26a-b, 29, 30, 31a-b

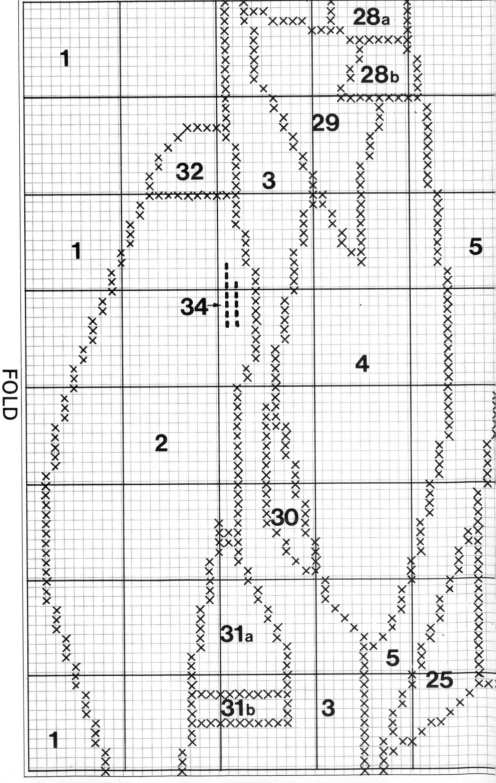

SELVAGE TOP AND BOTTOM EDGES

Color	Stitch	Shape Number
Dark purple	Cross Stitch	5, 8
Plum	Cross Stitch	3, 11, 17, 22, 23, 33
Cream	Cross Stitch	14, 19, 20, 27, 28a–b, 32

Stitch diagram shows outline of shapes as they appear on grid of canvas, each square representing one stitch. Larger grid is colored guidelines woven into canvas. Tracings should be made from this diagram.

Stitch and color chart

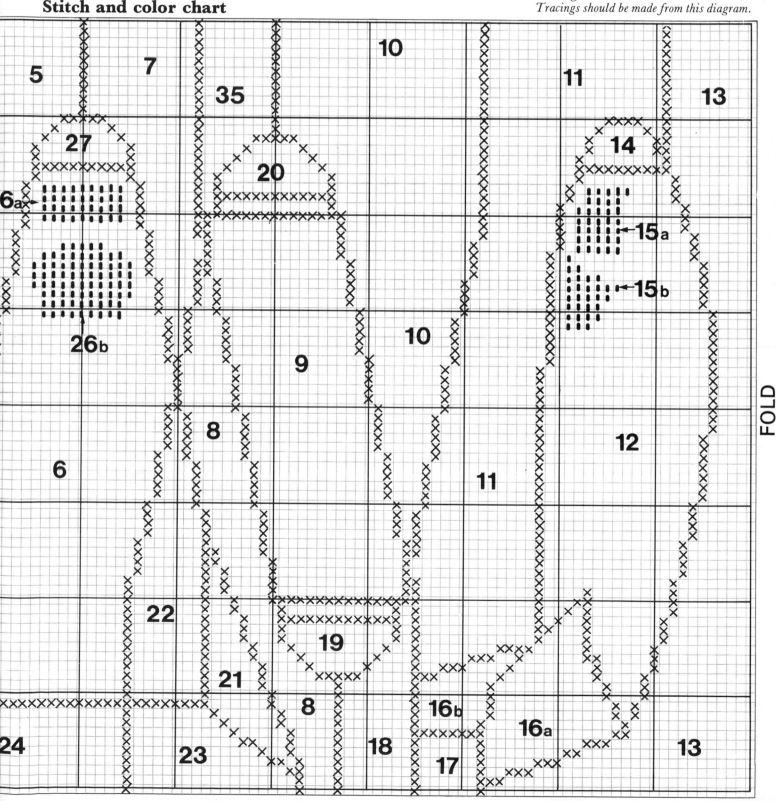

FOLD

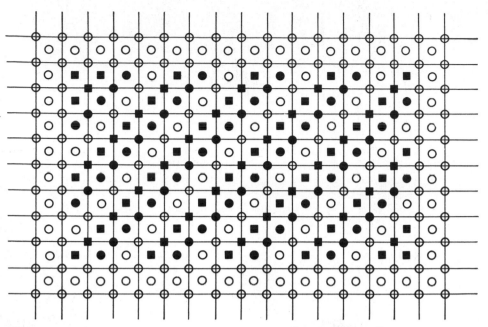

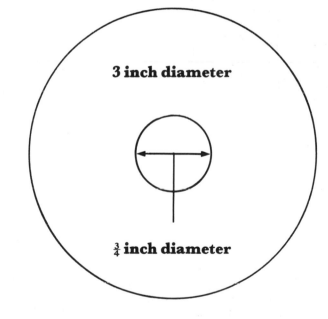

3 inch diameter

¾ inch diameter

○ **A, Plum**

■ **B, Burnt Orange**

● **C, Scarlet**

One of the above squares equals one 3 inch square on canvas

Winding the yarn around the card

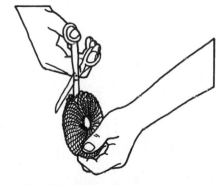

Cutting the yarn

Pompon rug

Pompons are great fun to make and require no special skills. This unusual rug is made from lots of brightly colored pompons sewn onto a canvas backing to make a gay and unusual rug.

Materials required
To make a rug measuring 33 inches by 51 inches you will need:
Using rug skeins:
70 2 ounce skeins in A, Plum
24 2 ounce skeins B, Burnt Orange
22 2 ounce skeins C, Scarlet

1 yard 60 inches wide stenciled canvas

Large bodkin

Piece of cardboard 7 inches by 4 inches

Each skein makes 3 pompons. Adjust quantity accordingly if a different size rug is required

Tension for this design
Each pompon measures 3 inches in diameter

To make the pompons
Cut two circles of cardboard, each 3 inches in diameter and with a hole in the center, from the template given here. Cut a skein into 3 pieces – each about 7⅔ yards in length – and thread one length into the bodkin.

Thread the yarn through the center hole of the two pieces of card taken together as one, over the cardboard and up through the center again. Continue winding the yarn around the cardboard in this way, covering it evenly until only 6 inches of yarn remains. Cut through the outer edge of the yarn between the two circles of cardboard. Wind the 6 inches length tightly around all the yarn where it passes through the center of the cards. Secure and leave the end for sewing on.

To complete
Make 210 pompons using A, 71 in B and 66 in C.

Sew pompons to canvas as shown in chart, using the remainder of the 6 inch end, and leaving 3 inches between the center of each of the pompons.

Trim the canvas two ½ inch from outer pompons.

Multi-colored braided rugs

For maximum impact at minimum cost, braid yourself a hard-wearing rag rug. This old cottagers' technique may be called 'poor man's loom', but the effect is a rich explosion of color which can be as haphazard or as planned as you please.

Rugs of this sort can be made of any scrap materials from wool skeins to old tights. A warm oval rug of the type shown here made from scraps of tweed, would look good in front of the fire, by the bed or inside the front door.

You may be able to get hold of some bags of scraps from a clothing manufacturer – otherwise it's worth looking through shapeless, unloved tweed and woolen clothes at second-hand sales for rock-bottom bargains.

Materials required

To make this oval, multicolored rug measuring 3 feet by 2 feet you will need:

Tweed and wool scraps adding up to about 8 yards by 36 inches.

Thread, sewing needle and bodkin.

Plaiting the rug

Cut the fabric into strips 3 inches wide. Turn under the edges and fold (Fig. 1). It is best to press these into position and then keep them folded by pinning them or by winding them around pieces of cardboard.

Join two pieces of the braid together using a bias seam and snip the corner off (Fig. 2). Attach the third folded strip with a few stitches to form a T (Fig. 3). Secure this end to a hook or door handle so that both hands are free for braiding.

Start by bringing the left-hand strip over the center strip and then the right-hand strip over that (Fig. 4). Continue braiding, making sure that the folded edges are kept towards the center of the braid. Keep the tension even, neither too tight nor too loose, and push the work up against the already braided end.

As you finish a strip, join on a new one with a bias seam. It is best if the lengths you work with are uneven so that the seams will not all fall in one place.

If the colors are predominantly muted, with only the occasional bright touch, try to space out the bright pieces. Otherwise, work all the colorful pieces together to make a band a little way in from the edge.

Making up

Lacing is the easiest and strongest method of connecting braids. Thread a blunt tapestry needle or bodkin with either carpet thread or strong waxed cotton. Draw it through the loop of one braid then thread through the corresponding loop of the braid opposite.

Wind the braid round and round, keeping it flat and not too tight or too loose. Ease in the curves to keep the work flat.

On an oval rug, such as this, make the first braided length of 12 inches and fold in half. Then lace to give a long shaped center. Wind the remaining braid around this easing in the fullness where necessary.

As you approach the end of the rug, start to taper the strips to diminish the size of the braid so that it will gradually blend into the last braided row of the rug. Weave the remaining ends of the braid into the outer ring of the work – you may find a crochet hook helpful here. Slipstitch the ends invisibly to secure in place.

You may wish to line or back the finished work if so choose a non-slip fabric. Cut the backing to the shape of the rug, allowing $\frac{1}{2}$ inch to $\frac{3}{4}$ inch for turnings. Slip stitch edges to back.

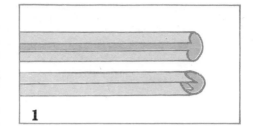
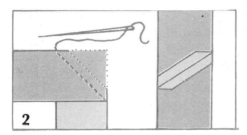
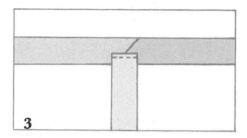
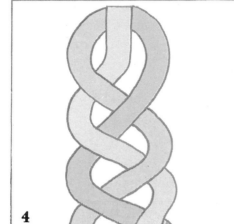

1 *Turning under the fabric edges*
2 *Joining two strips*
3 *Forming a 'T' with the third strip*
4 *Braiding the rug*
5 *Lacing the braids together*
6 *Weaving the ends of the braid into the outer ring of the rug, using a crochet hook*

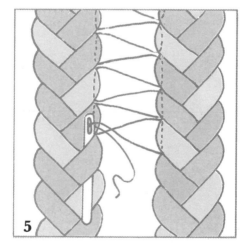

Bright scraps of material have been used in coils for this attractive multi-colored rug.

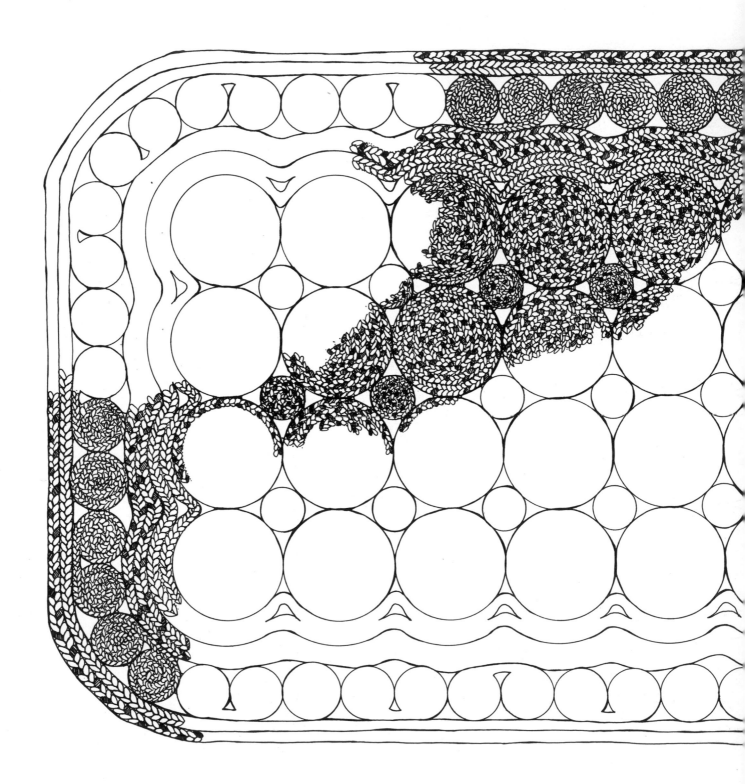

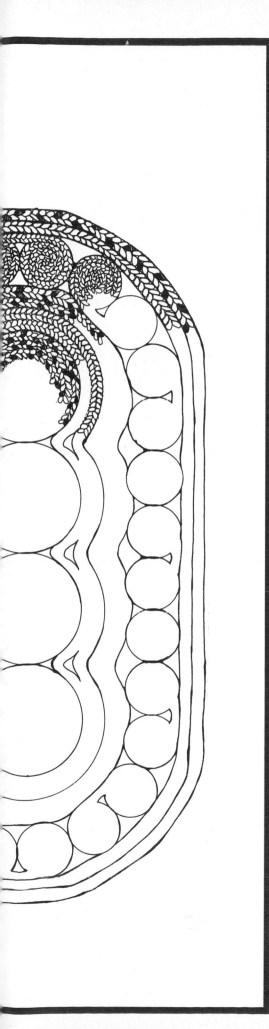

Braided wool rugs

Braided rugs made from hanks of wool have the advantages of allowing you to be able to choose your own color scheme, although they often involve more expense.

Materials required

2 ounce balls of Spinnerin rug wool in the following colors and amounts:

Six balls 6841 orange; five balls each of pale olive and dark olive; three balls each of 6847 half pink, 6816 aqua, 6843 yellow, 6003 light lime.

Two balls each of 6813 true red, 6817 pearl, 6800 white, 6884 plum, blue.

One ball each of dark red, 6874 wedgewood, 6834 navy.

Making up

To make the braids, cut threads of wool to different lengths, between 23½ inches and 47 inches. Braid them together using the strands double, mingling the various colors.

To make the circles coil up the braids and stitch them on the reverse side. Make the circles in two sizes, 24 larger ones with a 7 inch diameter and 15 smaller ones with a 7 inch and 15 smaller ones with a 3 inch diameter. Lay out the colored circles in the shape of the rug then stitch them together.

Next sew two red braids around the outside edge, followed by two multi-colored braids. Make red circles 4¼ inches in diameter, then double circles of pale and dark olive, 3½ inches in diameter. Stitch the final braids of green and red around the outer edge to complete.

Below A brilliantly-colored braided rug *made up of coils of braided strands of wool and finished with bright red and lime green braiding.*

Traditional rag rug

Create your own original and inexpensive rugs. All you need to make these colorful rugs are an old or worn blanket and scraps and odd pieces of fabric.

Materials required to make the rug

Old or worn blanket

Scraps of heavy fabric or worn clothing

Button thread

To make the rug

If using a blanket that is completely worn in the center, cut out the worn part as shown (Fig. 1). Discard the center panel and place the four pieces together, with the outside edges to the center (Fig. 2).

Re-stitch the blanket together by machine, or overstitch the pieces together very firmly by hand.

To form the rug, cut the fabric pieces into strips, approximately $\frac{3}{4}$ inch wide and 12 inches long.

Using the button thread double, thread each strip as shown (Fig. 3), so that the tufts are approximately 2 inches deep. Alternatively, if the fabric pieces are too small to cut long strips, make strips of either 4 inches or 8 inches and thread them together as before, joining two or three pieces of fabric together to form the tufts.

Attach the tufts to the blanket using the button thread and forming tightly packed rows, approximately 1 inch apart (Fig. 4).

Completely cover the whole area so that no blanket can be seen, either through the tufts or around the edges.

1 *Cutting out the worn section*
2 *Repositioning the blanket pieces*
3 *Making the tufts*
4 *Placing the tufts on the blanket*

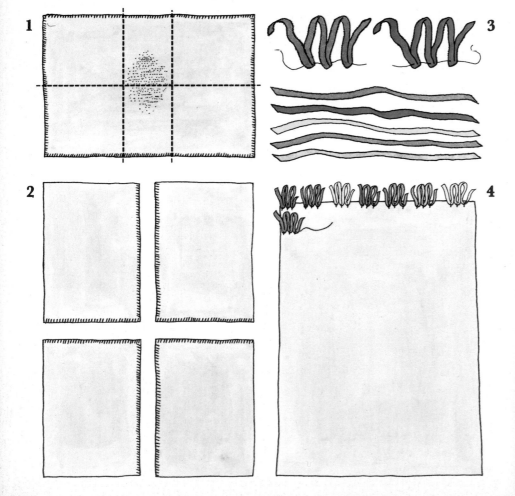

Patchwork rug from left-overs

An unusual and attractive patchwork rug can be made from leftover carpet, two or more old rugs or carpet sample books. When choosing a patchwork pattern it is best to select a design with large simple shapes and to avoid small or difficult shapes to cut. The rug shown has been made in a crooked-path pattern using three colors.

Materials required

To make a rug measuring 48 inches × 48 inches you will need: 36 inches × 36 inches of each color of carpet or rug or the equivalent of this in carpet squares.

47 inches × 47 inches of burlap

Adhesive

Handyman's knife

Heavy card for template

Ruler and felt-tip pen

Making the template

Draw the shape of an oblong 6 inches × 12 inches onto heavy card and cut out carefully.

Cutting out the patches

Place the template onto the back of the carpet and trace around it with a felt-tip pen. If the carpet has a heavy backing it may be necessary to grade the backing so that the pieces will fit closely together. Using a knife and ruler, cut out the patches in the appropriate colors.

Making the rug

Cut burlap to the required measurement.

Using the template trace the position of the patches onto the hessian. Position the carpet pieces onto the burlap making sure they fit as close together as possible.

Remembering to leave 2 inches free on all outer edges, glue down with adhesive. Allow to dry.

Finishing off

Fold the hem allowance over. Miter the corners as shown in the diagram. Glue the allowance down with adhesive on the wrong side. Glue the burlap to the edges of the carpet carefully and allow to dry.

Above *Chart to show the formation of the crooked path design. Try to keep to simple designs, as curves would make cutting more difficult.*

Crochet a durable rag rug

Bright crocheted rag rugs are now enjoying a revival in modern home decor. Made from torn strips as for the traditional rag rugs they are quick to make and easy to clean.

Tearing strips
Rugs are best made from cotton material torn in strips about ¾ inch wide. Tear the strips lengthwise from the fabric. The longer the piece of fabric the better.

Joining strips
If you are using leftover lengths of fabric you may be working with strips that are not very long. It saves time finishing the ends if both ends are laid along the top of the previous row for a few stitches and worked over using the new strip, so that they are held in place and are almost invisible. Any extra length can be trimmed away.

Materials required
To make a rug measuring 46 inches in diameter, you will need:
Strips of cotton ¾ inch wide in three colors (or rug wool may be used if you prefer)
A, Blue Green
B, Green
C, Yellow
One No.P (jumbo) crochet hook

Gauge
2sts to 1 inch over dc worked with No.P hook

Working the rug
Using No.P hook and A, work 6ch. Join with ss into first ch to form a circle.
1st round: 2ch, work 10dc into circles. Join with ss into 2nd of 2ch.
2nd round: Using B, *1sc between each of next 3dc, 1ch, rep from * to end. Join with ss to first sc.
3rd round: 2ch, *1sc into next sc, 1ch, rep from * to end. Join with a ss into first of 2ch.
4th round: Using C, 1ch, work 1sc into each st to end. Join with a ss into first ch.
5th round: Using A, 3ch, 2dc into next sc, *1dc into next sc, 2dc into next sc, rep from * to end. Join with a ss into 3rd of first 3ch.
6th round: Using C, 3ch, 1dc into each of next 2dc, 2dc into next dc, 1dc into each of next 3dc, rep from * to end. Join

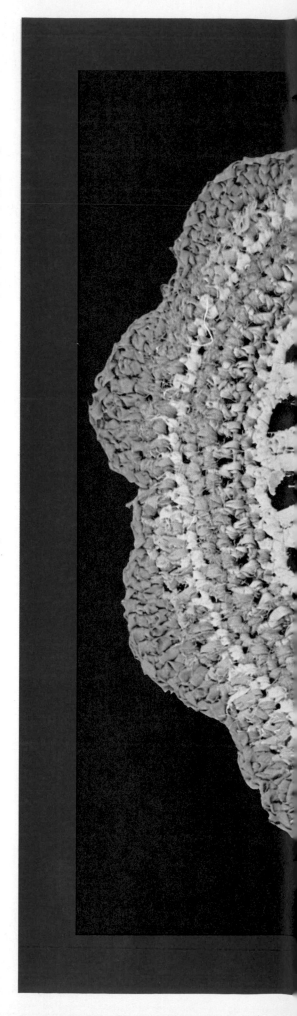

with a ss into 3rd of 3ch.
7th round: Using B, 1ch, 1sc into each st to end. Join with a ss into first ch.
8th round: *1sc into next sc, 1dc into next sc, 2dc into next sc, 1dc into next sc, rep from * to end. Join with a ss into first sc.
9th round: *1sc between 2sc of previous round, 1sc into next st, 2dc between each 3dc on previous round (3 groups of 2dc each), 1sc into next st, rep from * to end. Join with a ss into first sc.
10th round: Using A, join into center of point,*3sc into center st, 7ch, rep from * to end. Join with a ss into first st.
11th round: 3ch, 6dc into 7ch loop, 1dc into each 3sc, *7dc into 7ch loop, 1dc into each of next 3sc, rep from * to end. Join with a ss into 3rd of first 3ch.
12th round: 1ch, work 1sc into each dc. Join with a ss into first ch.
13th round: Using C, 1ch, work 1sc into each sc. Join with a ss into first ch.
14th round: 4ch, 1tr into next sc, 3ch, skip next 2sc, *1tr into each of next 2sc, 3ch, skip next 2sc, rep from * to end. Join with a ss into 4th of first 4ch.
15th round: Using C, join to first of 3ch with sc, 1sc into each of next 2ch, 1sc between 2tr, 4sc into ch loop, 1dc between 2tr, 1sc into each of next 3ch, 1sc between 2tr, 4sc into chain loop, 1dc between 2tr, rep from * to end. Join with a ss into first sc.
16th round: Using A, 1ch, work 1sc into each st. Join with a ss into first ch.
17th round: 3ch, *work 1dc into each sc. Join with a ss into 3rd of first 3ch.
18th round: Using B, 1ch, 1sc into each of next 4dc, *2sc into next dc, 1sc into each of next 5sc, rep from * to end. Join with a ss into first sc.
19th round: 1ch, work 1sc into every st. Join with a ss into first ch.
20th round: Using C, as 9th.
21st round: Using B, 3ch, 1dc into next 8sc, *2dc into next sc, 1dc into each of next 9sc, rep from * to end. Join with a ss into 3rd of first 3ch.
22nd round: 1ch, 1sc into next dc, 2dc into each of next 2dc, 2tr into each of next 3dc, 2dc into each of next 2dc, 1sc into each of next 2sc, *1sc into each of next 2dc, 2dc into each of next 2dc, 2tr into each of next 3dc, 2dc into each of next 2dc, 1sc into each of next 2sc, rep from * to end. Join with a ss into first ch. Finish off.

Circles and bands crochet rug

A simple and hardwearing rug suitable for a light and airy room can easily be crocheted using a cotton yarn. Worked in separate circles and bands, some pieces are crocheted together and some sewn.

Materials required
To make a rug 50 inch diameter you will need: 48 balls J. & P. Coats Speed-Srol-Sheen Crochet Cotton

One F or # 5 Aero crochet hook

Note Yarn is used double throughout

Tension
4sc to 1 inch
Small circle measures 5¼inch diameter.

Central Circle
Using an F or # 5 hook and double yarn begin at center, work 5ch. Join with a ss into first ch to form a circle.

1st round 1ch, 8sc into circle. Join with a ss into first ch.
2nd round 1ch, 1sc into same st, 2sc into each sc to end. Join with a ss into first ch. 18sc.
3rd round 1ch, 2sc into next sc, *1sc into next sc, 2sc into next sc, rep from * to end. Join with a ss into first ch. 27sc.
4th round 1ch, 1sc into next sc, 2sc into next sc, * 1sc into each of next 2sc, 2sc into next sc, rep from * to end. Ss into first ch. 36sc.
5th round 1 ch, 1sc into each sc to end. Join with a ss to first ch.
6th round 1 ch, 1sc into each of next 2sc, 2sc into next sc, * 1sc into each of next 3sc, 2sc into next sc, rep from * to end. Join with a ss into first ch.
7th round 1ch, 1sc into each of next 3 sc, 2sc into next sc, * 1sc into each of next 4sc, 2sc into next sc, rep from * to end. Join with a ss into first ch.
8th round 1ch, 1sc into each of next 4sc, 2sc into next sc, * 1sc into each of next 5sc, 2sc into next sc, rep from * to end. Join with a ss into first ch.
9th round 1ch, 1sc into each sc to end. Join with a ss into first ch.
10th round 1ch, 1sc into each of next 5sc, 2sc into next sc, *1sc into each of next 6sc, 2sc into next sc, rep from * to end. Join with a ss into first ch.

Continue working in rounds inc 9 times in each of every 3 rounds then working 1 round without inc, until work measures 20 inches across circle. Finish.

Small circles
Work as given for central circle from first to 9th rounds. Work 15 circles. Finish off ends. Join into a circle by sewing a few sts at sides of each circle together. Sew the base of each circle at equal intervals to central circle.

Band
Using an F or # 5 hook and double yarn join with a sc to center st at outside edge of any circle, 1sc into each of next 2sc towards left on same circle, 20ch, *1sc into 5 center sts at outside edge of next circle, 20ch, rep from * until all circles are joined, 1sc into each of 2 sts before joining st at beg of round.

Join with a ss into first sc.
Work in rounds as for central circle inc 9 times in each of 3 rounds and 1 round without inc, adjusting if necessary to keep mat flat. Work until band measures 4 inches. Join with a ss at each end of last round. Finish off.

Outer circles
Work as for central circle from first to 10th round. Finish off. Work 25 circles.

To make up
Finish off all ends.
Sew outer circles together into a circle as for inner circle and sew evenly to outside edge of band.
The wrong side of work is used as the right side of the mat.

Left An unusual crocheted rug worked using a cotton yarn double throughout. It would make an ideal addition to a bedroom or even for a kitchen as it is easy to clean and needs only a quick wash when dirty.
Below Chart to show the assembly of the rug. To complete the design you will need fifteen small circles for the inner ring and twenty-five larger circles for the outer ring.

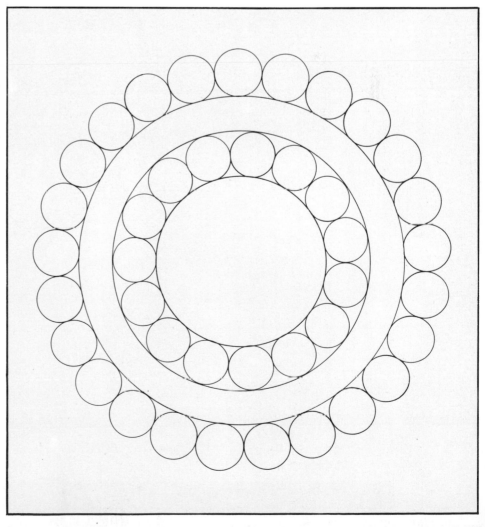

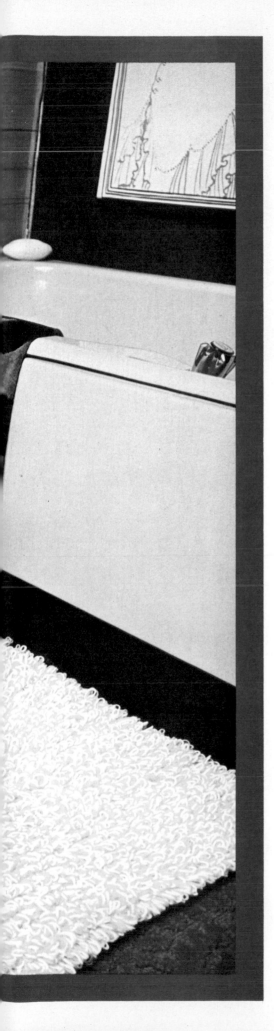

Bathroom set to crochet

Easy to wash. Quick to dry. Crochet this fresh-looking set for your bathroom.

Sizes
Bath mat: 18 inches by 24 inches
Pedestal mat: 18 inches by 24 inches
Seat cover: to fit average toilet seat

Gauge
12 sts and 12 rows to 4 inches over patt worked on G or #6 hook using yarn double.

Materials required
20 × 1 ounce balls knitting worsted in main shade, A
20 balls of contrast color, B
One E or #4 crochet hook
One G or #6 crochet hook
12 inch bias tape for seat cover

Bath mat
Using a G or #6 hook and one strand each of A and B together throughout, work 53ch loosely.
1st row Into 2nd ch from hook work 1sc, 1sc into each ch to end. Turn. 52sts.
2nd row *Insert hook into next st, (yo and wind around first finger of left hand) twice, yo and over finger once more and draw the 3 pairs of loops on the hook through the st, yo and draw through 3 pairs of loops on hook, yo and draw through rem 2 loops on hook – called one loop st –, rep from * to end of row. Turn.
3rd row Work 1sc into each st to end of row. Turn.
Note The normal one turning ch at the beg of every row has been omitted to give a firmer edge to the work.
Rep the 2nd and 3rd rows until work measures 24 inches from beg, ending with a 2nd row.
Fasten off.

Edging
Using an E or #4 hook and one strand each of A and B together, join to any corner and work 3sc into corner, cont all around outer edge of mat by working 1sc into each row end along the long sides, 3sc into each corner and 1sc into each st along the short sides. Join with a ss into first sc. Work one more round in sc.
Fasten off.

Pedestal mat
Work as given for bath mat until work measures 15 inches from beg, ending with a 2nd row.
Shape for pedestal
Next row Work 1sc into each of next 16 sts, turn.
Next row As 2nd row of patt.
Next row Work 1sc into each st to within last 2 sts, (insert hook into next st, yo and draw through a loop) twice, yo and draw through all hoops on hook – one st decreased. Turn.
Rep last 2 rows until 12sts rem. Cont without shaping until work measures 24 inches from beg. Fasten off.
Return to where work was left, miss first 20 sts in center, rejoin yarn to rem sts, work 1sc into each st to end. Turn.
Complete to match other side, reversing all shaping.
Edging Work as given for mat.

Seat cover
Using a G or #6 hook and one strand each of A and B together, work 11ch loosely.
1st row Into 2nd ch from hook work 1sc, 1sc into each ch to end. Turn. 10 sts.
2nd row As 2nd row of bath mat.
3rd row Work 2sc into first st, 1sc into every st to last st, 2sc into last st. Turn.
4th row Work 2 loop sts into first st, patt to last st, 2 loop sts into last st. Turn.
Rep last 2 rows until there are 40 sts. Cont to inc one st at each end of every foll 4th row until there are 44 sts. Work 7 rows without shaping. Dec one st at each end of next and every foll 4th row until 38 sts rem, then at each end of every foll alt row until 20 sts rem.
Fasten off.

Brim
With WS of work facing, using a G or #6 hook and one strand of A and B together, rejoin yarn to row end of 3rd row, work one loop st into each row end all around outer edge to within 2 row ends, turn.
Next row Work 1sc into each st all around. Turn.
Change to an E or #4 hook. Work 5 more rows in sc. Fasten off.
Cut tape in half and sew one piece to either side of open edges of brim.

For machine knitters— luxury underfoot

This sumptuous rug is specially designed for machine knitters who want to bring a touch of luxury to the living room or bedroom. It is made by a technique which is also useful for making smaller items such as cushions or trimming garments.

Knitting on a machine is not just a way of meeting the family's needs for classic sweaters, or of making fashionable garments for yourself. There are endless creative possibilities for knitting for the home as well, particularly if your machine can produce weaving techniques. This luxurious rug has a knitted backing, while the dense looped pile is woven in, working with two strands of yarn.

The rug can be worked to any required width up to the full width of the machine, and it can be made to any length.

The cushion has been worked with single strand loops. This gives a less dense, more floppy effect, which is also more economical. The rug could also be worked in this way.

Although specific instructions are given for the rug illustrated, it can easily be adapted by altering the dimensions, the yarn quality or the length of the loops. It is advisable, however, to use a thicker yarn for the loops than on the backing.

Materials required

To make a rug of the finished size 38 inches by 46 inches (excluding loops) you will need:

6 2 ounce balls of 4 ply yarn for backing (approximately 200 yards per ball)

94 2 ounce balls of Knitting worsted (1 ball should work about 470 loops)

1½ yards 30 inches wide iron-on backing fabric.

Tension for this design

7sts and 10 rows to 1 inch measured over plain st st worked in 4 ply. Each loop measures 2 inches.

Working the rug

Using the 4 ply yarn, cast on 200 sts. Knit 4 rows.

Set machine for weaving and put every second needle out of working position.

Make two loops of string, each using a length of about 6 inches, so that each loop measures exactly 2 inches. Hook one loop at each end of the needle bed and then hang the cast-on comb onto the loops.

Using Knitting worsted double throughout, take it over the first needle in the out of work position, down to the comb and hook the yarn under two teeth, up and over the second needle in the out of work position, down to the comb and round two teeth. Continue in this way along the row. Knit across the row to secure the loops. Knit one row without loops.

Put every other second needle (alternate to those in the previous loop row) into the out of work position and hook round the loops as before.

Continue in this way alternating a row of loops with a plain row of knitting until the required length is reached.

To finish off

Darn in the ends of the backing yarn and trim the ends of the loop yarn so that they are lost in the pile. Position adhesive backing onto the knitted backing, trimming as required. Press into place with a warm iron. Used in conjunction with a backing of this type, the loops are more secure from catching and being pulled.

Below *A detail of the looping on the finished rug. This is achieved by alternating a row of loops with a plain row of knitting until the desired length of rug is reached.*
Below left *Winding the loops around the comb. For the next row every other second needle (alternate to those of the first row) should be put into the out of work position.*

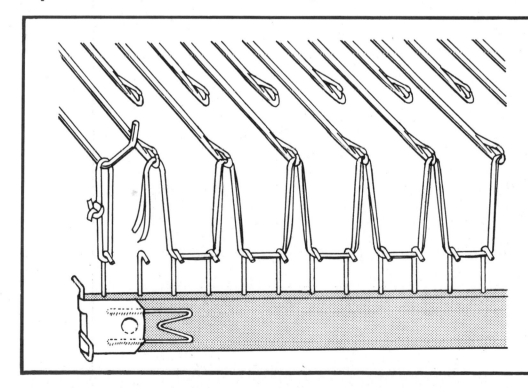

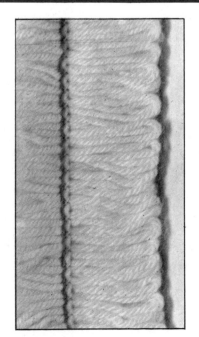

Key to applique areas
Sea – Turquoise colored fabric
Roads – Beige webbing
Airport runway – Orange felt
Grass – Green felt

Hangar – Maroon and pink felt
Fields – Dark brown, mid brown and green felt
Gardens – Flowered fabric scraps
Houses – Different colored felts

Trees – Brown felt for trunks, green felt for foliage, fruit from various colored felts.
Treasure island – Sand brown, green and orange felt

Play plan

This play-plan rug is made of burlap, fabric, felt appliqué and embroidery and, although it is major sewing project, would make a superb and long-appreciated gift for a child. Follow the key for the major areas on the plan. The rug could also be made up as a wall hanging by sewing 1 inch brass rings along one edge on the wrong side.

Materials required

To make the rug measuring 36 inches by 54 inches you will need: $1\frac{1}{2}$ yards 72 inches wide burlap, in deep sea green

6 yards 1 inch wide wool braid, in navy

Rickrack braid: 2 yards white, 3 yards emerald, $1\frac{1}{2}$ yards yellow, $\frac{1}{2}$ yard red

4 yards $\frac{1}{4}$ inch wide white tape

8 yards $1\frac{1}{2}$ inches wide beige webbing

Guipure lace daisy edging: 2 yards white, $\frac{1}{2}$ yard pink

$\frac{1}{2}$ yard 36 inches wide felt, orange

12 inch squares felt in dark brown, mid brown, maroon, lime green, leaf green, apricot, flesh pink, pale yellow, cerise pink and sand brown

Scraps of felt in red, gray, olive green and white

Scraps of four flowered fabrics

Thin foam, 36 inches by 54 inches

Soft embroidery thread in white, beige and pink

Fabric adhesive

To make the rug

Cut the burlap into two pieces, each 36 inches by 54 inches. Bind the raw edges of one piece with narrow adhesive tape to prevent fraying. Keep the remaining piece for backing the completed rug.

Major pieces are pinned, basted and stitched in place one at a time. Cut out the sea from turquoise fabric, allowing plenty of underlap to go beneath bridges and beaches.

Machine stitch in place, using zig-zag stitch if possible or a straight machine stitch $\frac{1}{8}$ inch from the edge.

To complete the rug

Remove the adhesive tape binding. Press the rug lightly.

Dab adhesive over one side of the backing burlap. Smooth the foam padding over the glued side of the burlap, working from the center towards the edges. Dab adhesive over the foam.

Place the rug over the foam, right side up, and tack around the edges through all three thicknesses. Press the wool braid in half lengthwise, baste one edge over the right side of the rug, mitering corners. Stitch.

Turn the other edge of the braid over to the wrong side of the rug, slipstitch. Cut the remaining braid into four equal lengths. Make loops and stitch them to the wrong side of one long edge.

Use the loops to hang the rug on the wall when not in use, or stitch on brass rings.

Below *Color chart for the rug showing the position of the applique areas.*

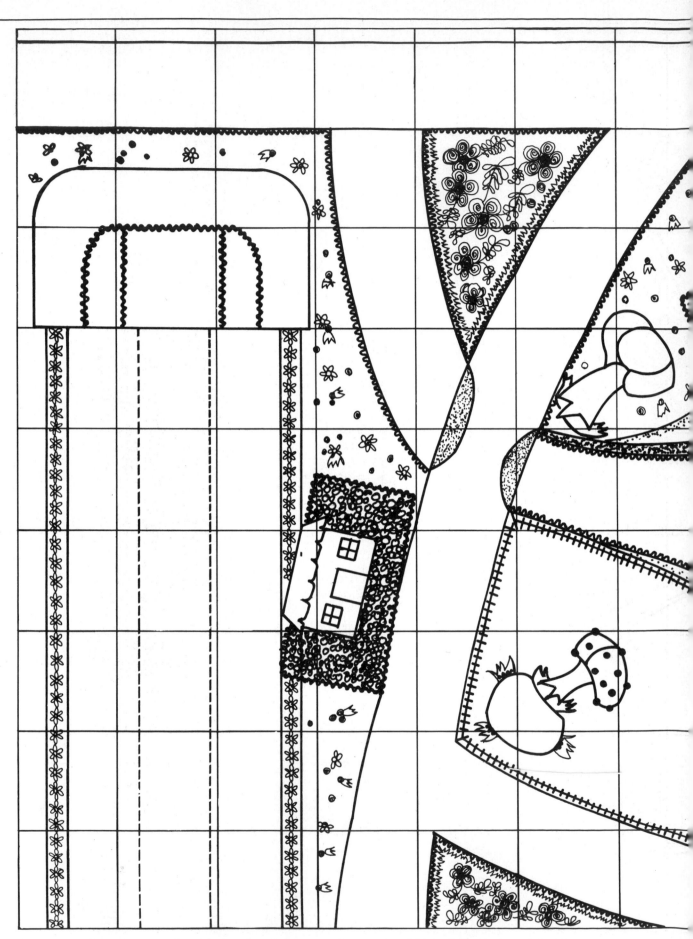

Graph pattern for the floor play plan. Draw each square up to 2 inches to make a full-sized floor rug or wall hanging. Work to a smaller scale for a table top game for a child to color.

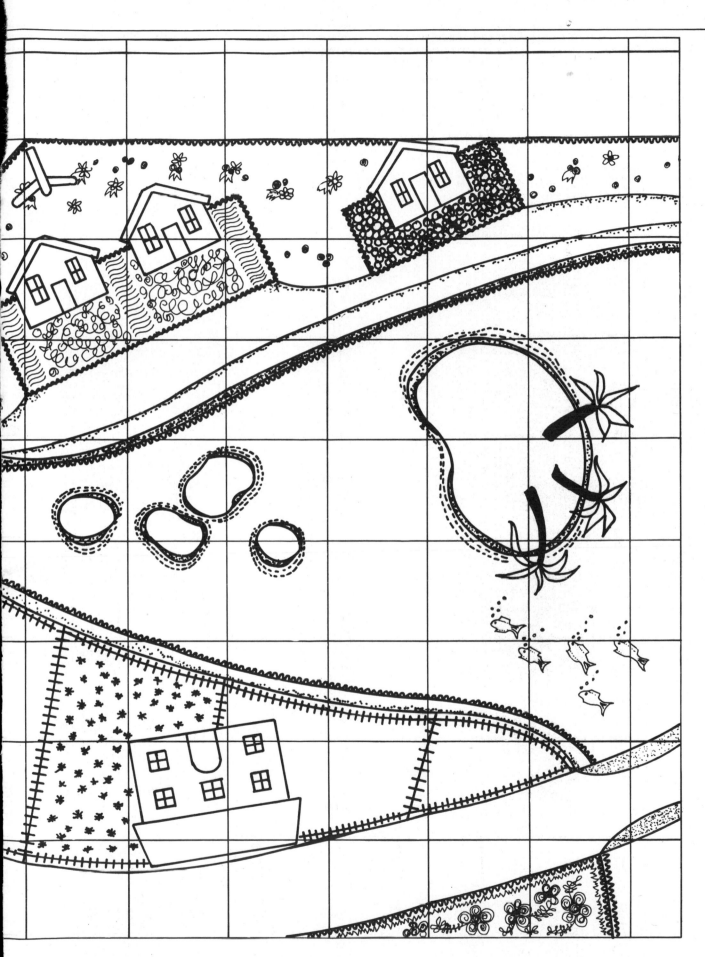

1 square = 2 inches

Catch a tiger

This eye-catching tiger may be fake but he's fun. Made out of fur fabric, it can be used as a cover or a rug to brighten up a bedroom or playroom.

Materials required

To make the rug to fit an average size single bed you will need:

2 yards of 54 inches wide fur fabric

Small quantities of brown, black and dark pink felt.

$\frac{3}{4}$ inch diameter fish-eye buttons

1 bag kapok or other stuffing

Fabric adhesive

Black felt-tipped pen (colorfast)

Thread to match fur fabric

Linen carpet thread to match fabric and in black

Large eyed long needle

Small quantity black wool

Small piece cardboard

Making the pattern

Using graph paper draw the main pattern pieces to scale. One square = 1 square inch. Trace the pieces for the nose, eyes and tongue to the exact size.

An allowance of ¼ inch has been made on all seams and for the hem. Cut out the pattern pieces and mark all notches, dots and the straight grain line.

Cutting out

Following the cutting layout, fold the fur fabric and place the pieces forming the body, head, cheeks, ear, tail and paw facings onto it. Pin into place and cut out. Transfer the markings from the pattern pieces to the fabric. From the brown felt, cut out the pieces for the nose and to cover the cardboard for the eyes.

From the pink felt cut the piece for the tongue.

Making the rug

Head: with right sides facing join the center-fronts and backs leaving an opening at the center-back between the dots. With right sides facing and matching the balance marks, join the back to the front. Turn right side out.

Stuff the head, using about half the stuffing. Slipstitch the opening together.

Cheeks: with right side facing, join the pieces for the cheeks at the center-front. Press open the seam with your fingers.

Using the matching carpet thread,

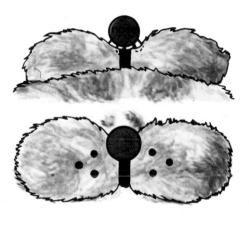

work large overcasting stitches over the outside edge of the cheeks. Turn the cheeks on to the wrong side, place some stuffing in the center and pull up the overcasting stitches until the cheeks measure approximately 8½ inches long by 3½ inches wide.

Wind black wool over the center-front, and pull tightly and fasten off securely on the wrong side. Place the cheeks into the position indicated on the face and slipstitch firmly into place using heavy thread.

Nose: work a row of overcasting round the outside edge. Turn the nose wrong side up, place some stuffing in the center and pull up the overcasting stitches to form a ball. Place the nose on to the cheeks, positioning it at the top of the black wool. Slipstitch the nose neatly into place.

Punch out or cut out six small dots from the black felt and stick in place on to the cheeks with adhesive.

Tongue: with the right side facing the head, place the tongue on to the head so that the fold line is just below the bottom of the cheeks. Stitch along the fold line. Spread a little adhesive on to the under piece of the tongue, fold the top piece over on to it and press together.

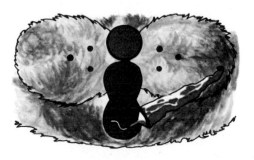

Ears: with right sides facing and matching balance marks, join the two pieces for each ear round the outside curved edges. Turn right side out.

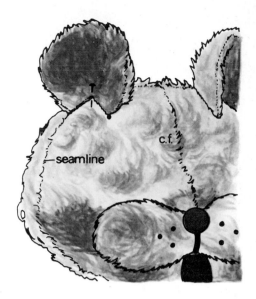

Fold under the turnings on the straight edges and slipstitch together. Mark the center of the straight edges with a pin. Place the pin on to the seam line of the head in the position indicated. Sew on the ears at the angle shown.

Eyes: from the right side, work a row of overcasting round the pieces for the eyes. Turn them to the wrong side and place the card pieces in the middle. Pull up the overcasting stitches tightly and fasten off. Place the buttons in the center of the right side and stitch in place with the black linen thread. Work some stitches through to the back of the head and pull tightly to depress the face at the eyes. To make the eyes more realistic, fill in the groove of the button with the black felt-tipped pen.

The body: fold the neck edge turning of the body on to the right side and machine stitch down. Fold the running of the straight edge of the facings on to the wrong side and machine stitch.

With the right sides together, stitch the facings to the paws and tail round the curved edge. Turn right side out and fill with remaining stuffing.

Hem the straight edge of the facings to the wrong side of the body. Fold the remaining hem round the edge of the body on to the wrong side and stitch as near to the edge as possible if you are using a straight stitch machine, or with a wide long zig-zag stitch on a zig-zag machine.

Place the head on to the body so that 2½ inches extends over the neck edge. Slipstitch all round. Finish off by teasling the face, paws and tail with a teasle, poodle brush or stiff hair brush.

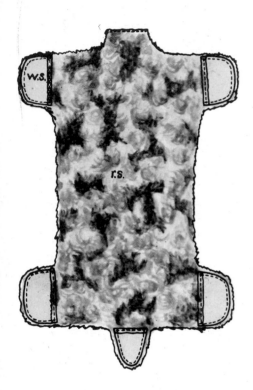

Right *Graph pattern for the tiger rug. Using 1 inch squared graph paper, draw up an enlarged pattern, square by square, following all lines and curves.*

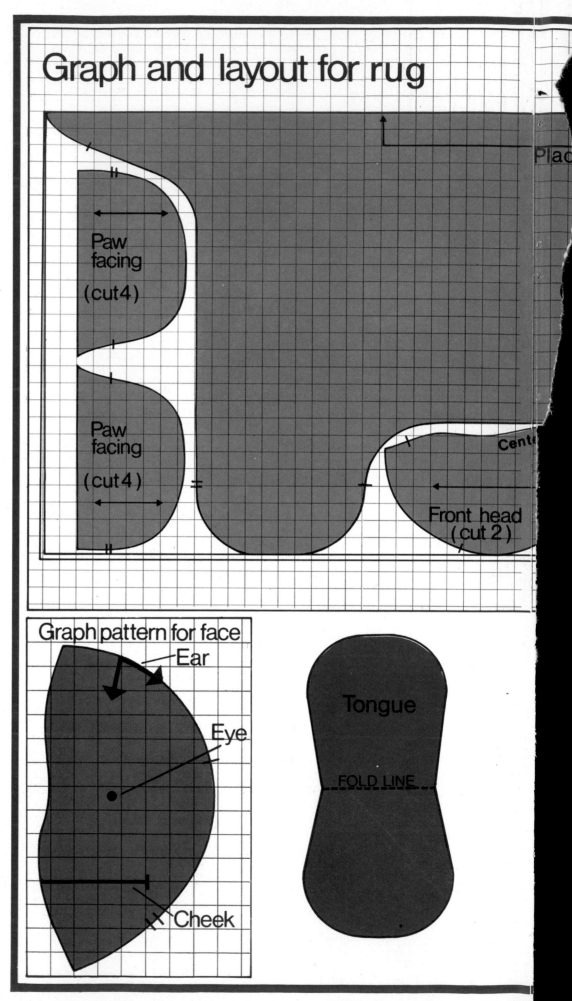

Graph and layout for rug

Paw facing
(cut 4)

Paw facing
(cut 4)

Front head
(cut 2)

Plac

Cent

Graph pattern for face

Ear

Eye

Cheek

Tongue

FOLD LINE

84

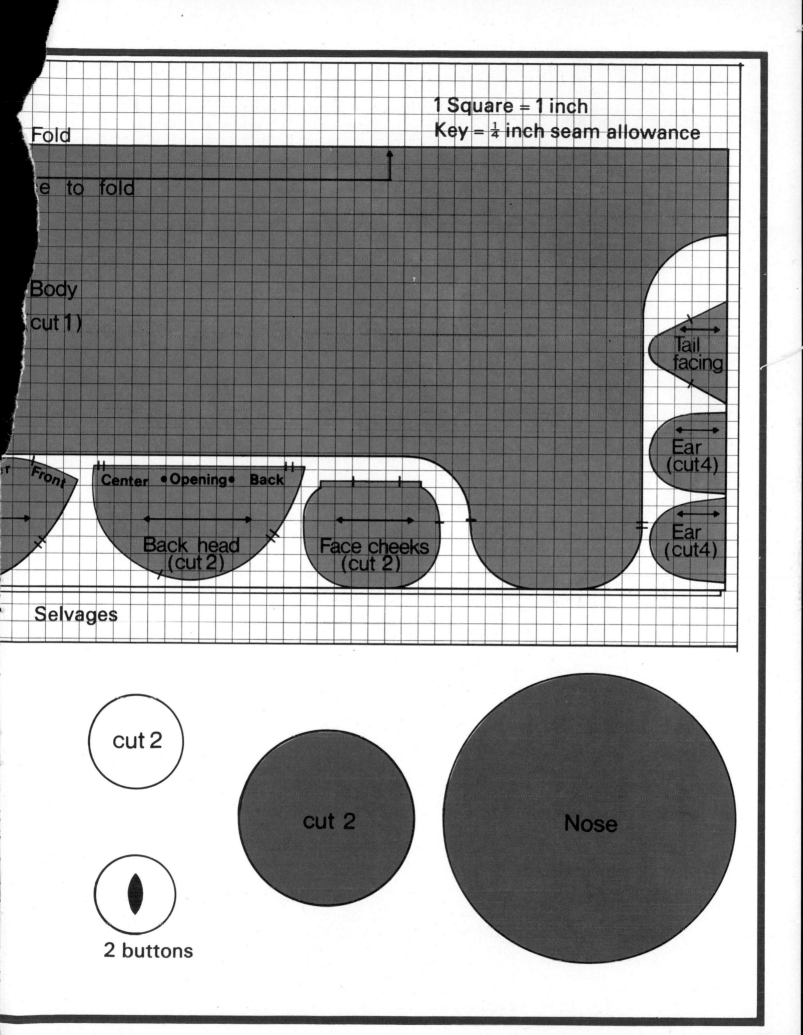

1 Square = 1 inch
Key = $\frac{1}{4}$ inch seam allowance

Fold

e to fold

Body

(cut 1)

Tail facing

Ear (cut 4)

Front

Center • Opening • Back

Back head (cut 2)

Face cheeks (cut 2)

Ear (cut 4)

Selvages

cut 2

2 buttons

cut 2

Nose

Crochet square rug

A warm and beautiful crochet rug makes an ideal addition to any bedroom. Made out of crochet squares, a whole bedroom set, including the bedspread, can be made to match.

Materials required

To make a rug of the finished size 26 inches by 48 inches you will need:
8 2-ounce balls of tweed Knitting worsted in main shade, A
2 balls in contrast color, B
3 balls in contrast color, C

One I or 9 crochet hook

To make square motifs

Using 1 or 9 hook and B, make 6ch. Join with a ss to first ch to form circle.

1st round 3ch, *(yo, insert hook into circle and draw through a loop, yo and draw through one loop, yo and draw through 2 loops), twice, yo and draw through all 3 loops on hook, *, (5ch, (yo, insert hook under ch and draw through a loop, yo and draw through 1 loop, yo and draw through 2 loops) 3 times, yo and draw through all 4 loops on hook – called 1C1 –, 2ch, 1C1 into circle) 3 times, 5ch, 1C1 into circle, 2ch. Join with a ss to 3rd of first 3ch. Break off B. Join in A.

2nd round: Using A, rejoin yarn into any 5ch sp, 3ch, rep from * to * of first round into same sp, 3ch, 1C1 into same sp, **2ch, 3dc into 2ch sp, 2ch. (1C1, 3ch, 1C1) into 5ch sp, rep from ** twice more, 2ch, 3dc into 2ch sp, 2ch. Join with a ss into 3rd of first 3ch. Break off A. Join in C.

3rd round: Using C, rejoin yarn into any 3ch sp, 3ch, rep from * to * of first round into same sp, 3ch, 1C1 into same sp, **2ch, 2dc into 2ch sp, 1dc into next 3dc, 2dc into 2ch sp, 2ch, (1C1, 3ch, 1C1) into 3ch sp, rep from ** twice more, 2ch, 2dc into 2ch sp, 1dc into each of next 3dc, 2dc into 2ch sp, 2ch. Join with a ss to 3rd of first 3ch. Break off C. Join in A.

4th round: Using A, rejoin yarn into any 3ch sp, 3ch, rep from * to * of first round into same sp, 3ch, 1C1 into same sp, **2ch, 2dc into 2ch sp, 1dc into each of next 7dc, 2dc into 2ch sp, 2ch (1C1, 3ch, 1C1) into 3ch sp, rep from ** twice more, 2ch, 2dc into 2ch sp, 1dc into each of next 7dc, 2dc into 2ch sp,

2ch. Join with a ss to 3rd of first 3ch. Fasten off.

Making up

Make 28 square motifs and press on wrong side under a damp cloth with a warm iron. To join, place two squares right sides together and stitch in 4 strips of 7 squares. Then join these strips together.

Edging

Using I or #9 hook, A and with wrong side of work facing, rejoin yarn.

1st round: 2ch, 1hdc into each st, picking up back loop only, working 1ch at each seam and 3hdc into each corner. Join with a ss into 2nd of first 2ch.

Next round: 2ch, 1hdc into each st, picking up both loops, working 1hdc into each ch sp and 3hdc into each corner. Join with a ss to 2nd of first 2ch.

Next round: 2ch, 1hdc into each st picking up back loops only and working 3hdc into each corner. Join with a ss to 2nd of first 2ch. Fasten off. Press seams. Press edging.

Working the fringe

Make a fringe at each end of rug by cutting yarn into 11 inch lengths and knotting 3 strands into every other stitch along each short end. Trim fringe so that ends are even.

To make a matching bedspread you will need 154 square motifs measuring 70 inches by 228, joined in 11 strips of 14. Then these strips are joined together. Follow instructions for edging as for rug.

Below *Once the basic idea for the squares has been grasped, it is quite simple to adapt them to create a soft-and homey matching bedroom set.*

Techniques for rug design

Inspiration for rug designs can come from many places. Books and magazines arc an obvious source but equally posters, prints or even a sketch of a country scene can be adapted to fit a rug canvas. It is often wise to avoid really intricate designs as the scale on which you are working would destroy some of the subtleties, especially with hooked and rya rugs. With stitched rugs these designs are far more successful. However, simple stylized designs are often far more effective and much cheaper to work.

Enlarging and reducing designs

Whether you are using your own design or some pattern or illustration which you like, you will often need to enlarge or reduce it to fit the size you need. This is easy to do if you divide the design into little squares and divide the area where you want it enlarged into the same amount of squares. You will find you can easily copy each square individually and so build up the whole design. You can reduce a design in just

Below *Inspiration for rug designs can be gleaned from many sources. This design can easily be enlarged for a rug.*

the same way, but copying onto smaller squares.

To avoid marking the original design, and to save the bother of drawing out lots of little squares, transfer the design onto graph paper. To do this, you can either trace it direct, if the graph paper is thin enough or use tracing paper.

Trace the design onto tracing paper (Fig 1). Lay this over graph paper. If you can see the squares clearly through the tracing paper, stick it down with clear tape, being careful that the tracing paper lies flat. This way, you can re-use the graph paper.

If, however, you cannot see the squares clearly through the tracing, transfer the design to the graph paper either with carbon paper (dressmaker's carbon is fine) or by shading the back of the tracing paper with a soft pencil and drawing firmly over the design with a ballpoint.

Draw a rectangle to enclose the design (Fig 2). This will be divided into a certain number of squares by the graph paper. If you are using plain paper you must, at this stage, divide the rectangle up by marking off each side and joining up the marks to make a lot of small squares. It is helpful to number these for reference.

Next draw, preferably on tracing paper as before, a second rectangle, to the size you want the finished design to be and in the same proportions as the first one. Do this by tracing two adjacent sides of the first rectangle and the diagonal from where they meet. Extend them as much as you need and then draw in the other sides of the second rectangle (Fig 3). Divide this into the same number of squares as the smaller one. A backing sheet of graph paper will make this process easier.

Carefully copy the design square by square. If you have to copy a flowing, curved line across several squares, mark the points at which it crosses the squares and then join them up in one flowing movement (Fig 4).

Transferring your design onto the canvas is much simpler in rug-making than with other crafts. Having drawn up your design to scale on squared paper, each square represents one knot. Taking colored pens simply color in on the paper your color scheme and work from this. You may prefer, especially on complicated designs, to actually fill in your color scheme on the canvas before beginning. For intricate needleworked rugs it is often far safer to work a sampler on canvas first to check your design. If it is a success, the sampler need not be wasted, but can always be made up into a cushion cover or a wall hanging.

One last point to remember. In a design where the pattern repeats itself there is no necessity to trace the whole design off but just the basic pattern for both rug and border.

Left *On patterns which have a repeat only one complete section need be traced up. This diagram shows the necessary segment for the design shown on the previous page.*
Below *Enlarging a design. 1 Draw the design on to tracing paper. 2 Draw a rectangle to enclose the design and number the squares in it. 3 Draw the second rectangle and diagonal. 4 Transfer the design.*

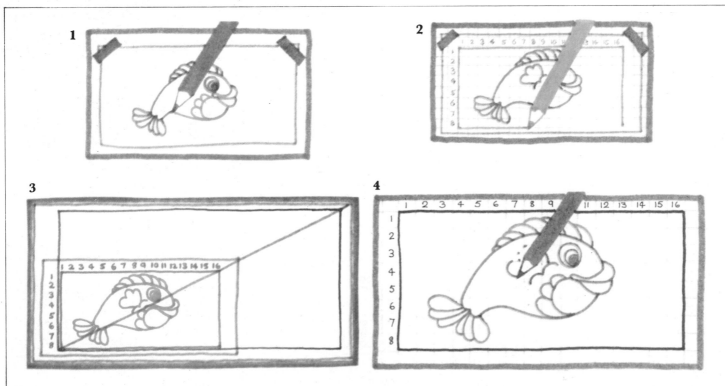